RECORDED VERSIONS
GUITAR

AUTHENTIC TRANSCRIPTIONS WITH NOTES AND TABLATURE

JEFF BECK BLOW BY BLOW

Music transcriptions by Pete Billmann, Aurelien Budynek, Jeff Jacobson, and David Stocker

ISBN 978-1-4234-9443-0

HAL•LEONARD®
CORPORATION

7777 W. BLUEMOUND RD. P.O. BOX 13819 MILWAUKEE, WI 53213

Visit Hal Leonard Online at
www.halleonard.com

CONTENTS

You Know What I Mean

By Jeff Beck and Max Middleton

A

Moderately ♩ = 101

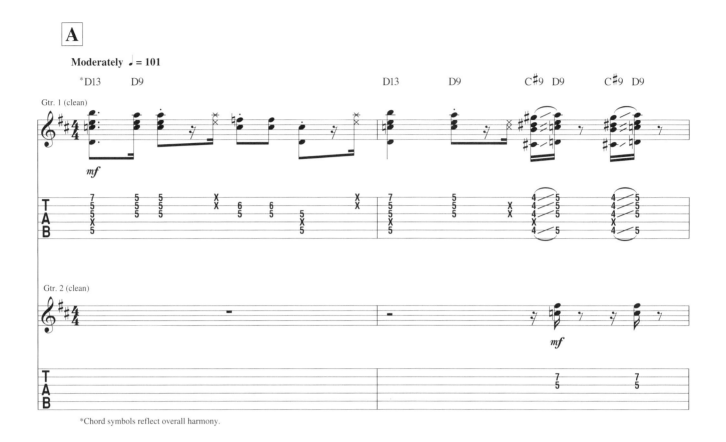

*Chord symbols reflect overall harmony.

*Harm. located approximately eight-tenths the distance between the 1st & 2nd frets.

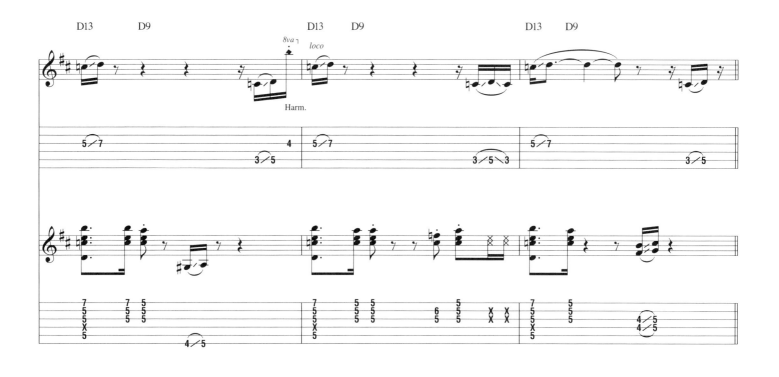

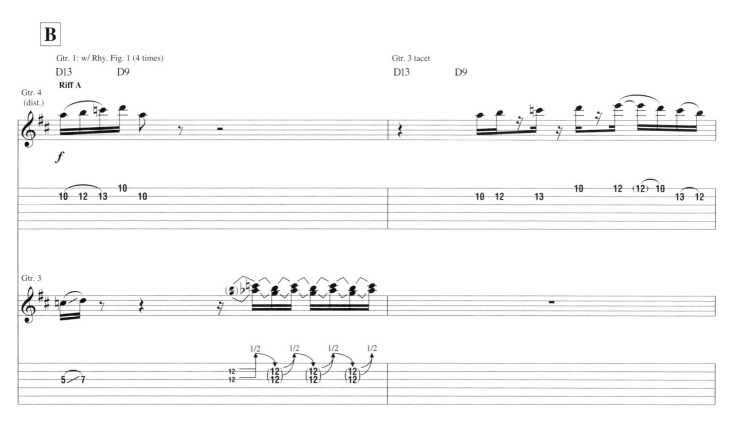

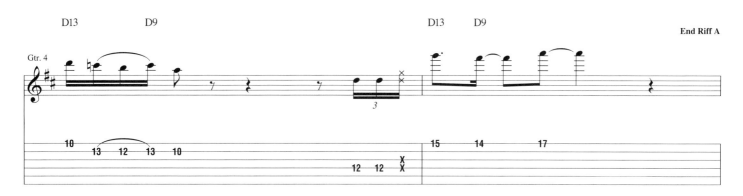

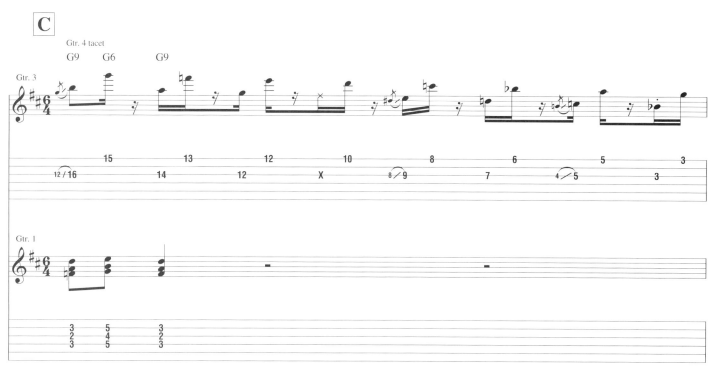

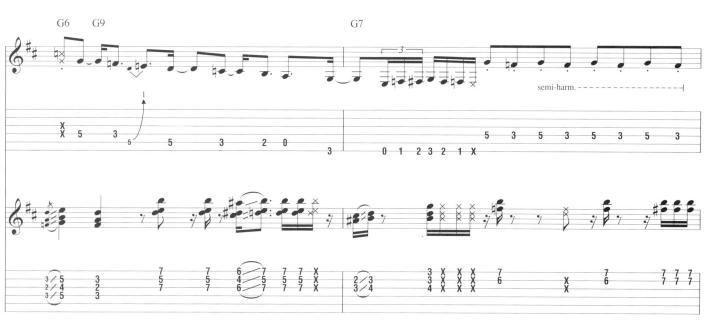

A

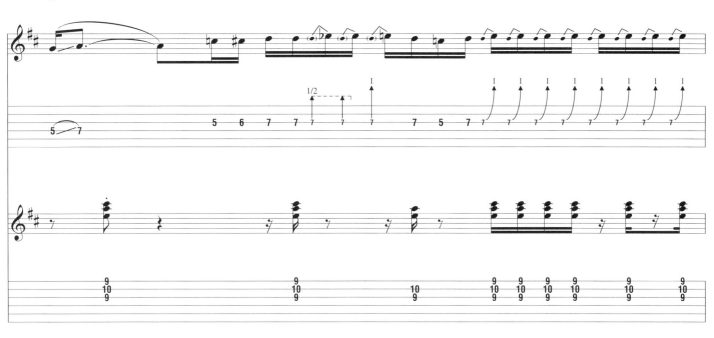

F   F# G

D

Gtr. 1: w/ Rhy. Fig. 1 (2 times)

D13   D9   D13   D9

Gtr. 3

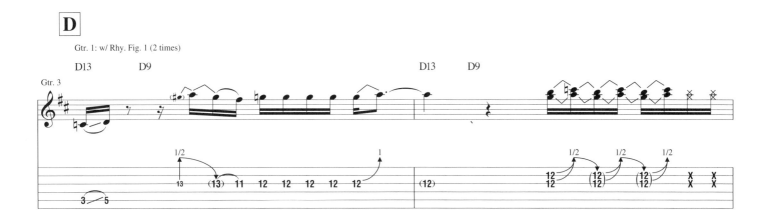

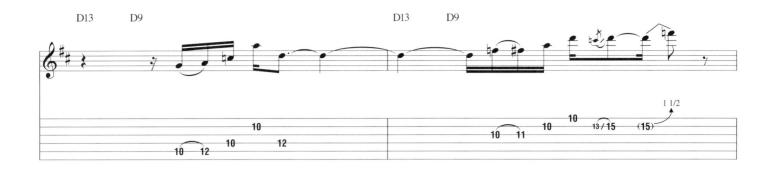

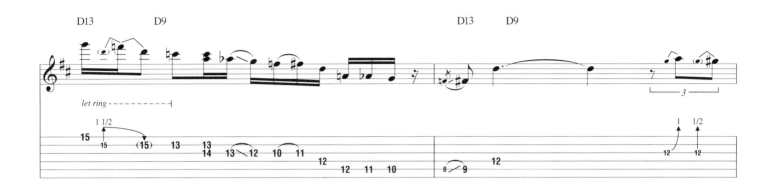

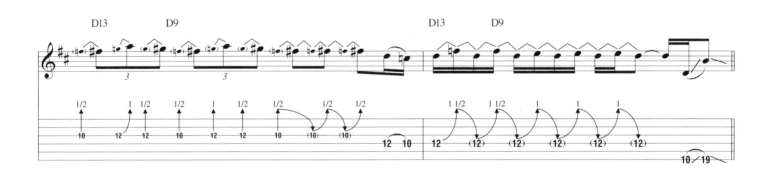

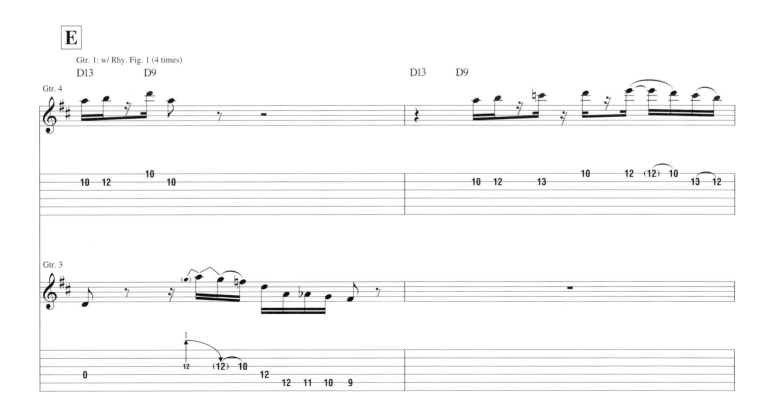

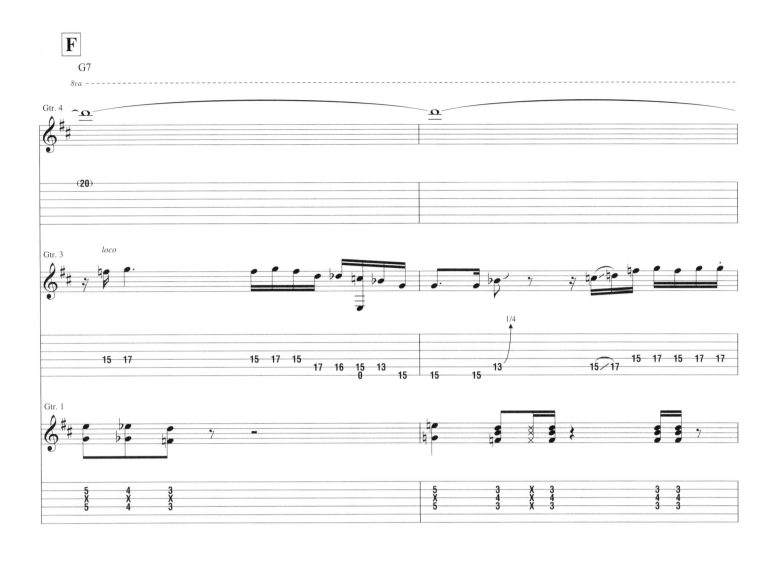

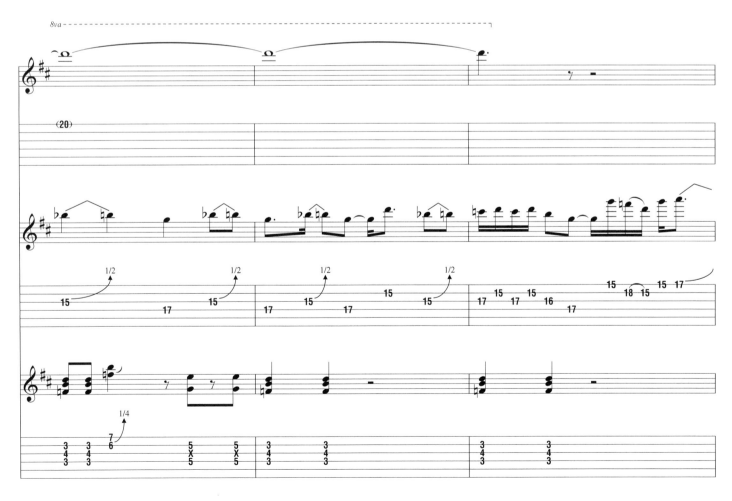

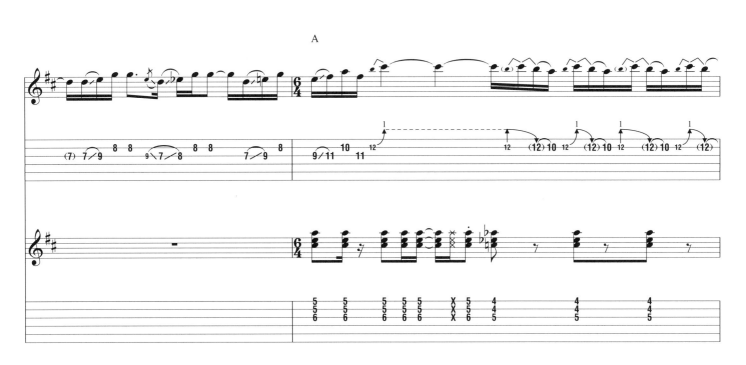

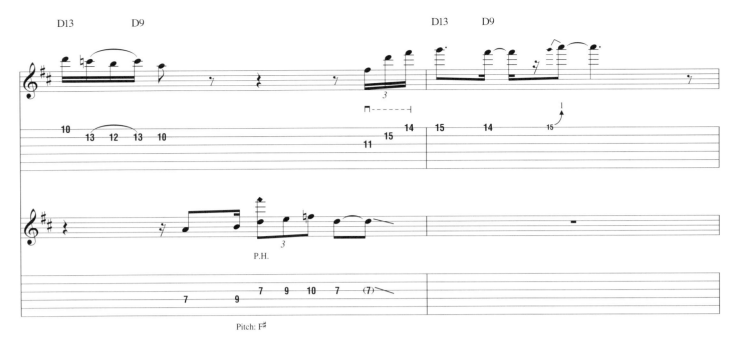

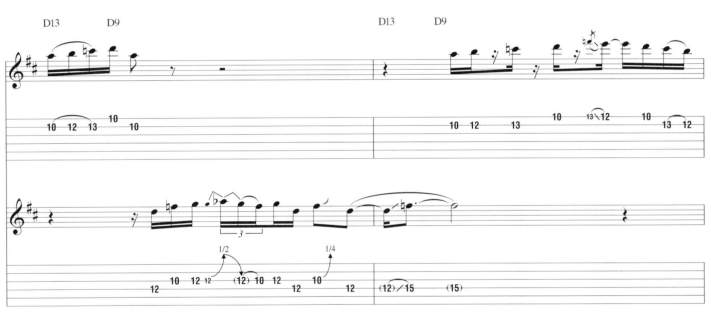

Segue to "She's a Woman"

Fade out

Begin fade

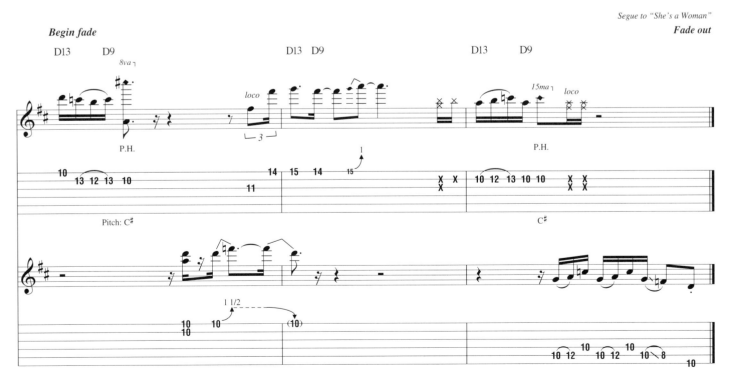

She's a Woman

Words and Music by John Lennon and Paul McCartney

I know __ that she's no peas - ant. __

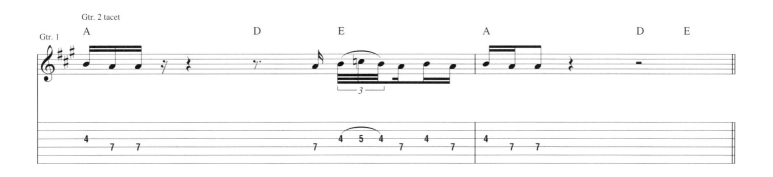

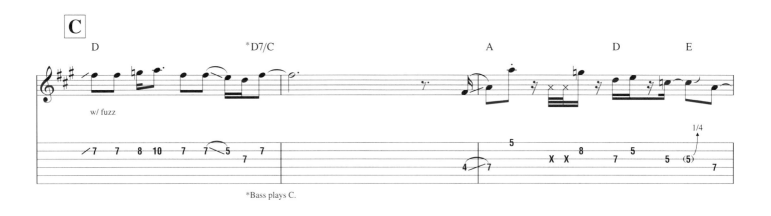

*Bass plays C.

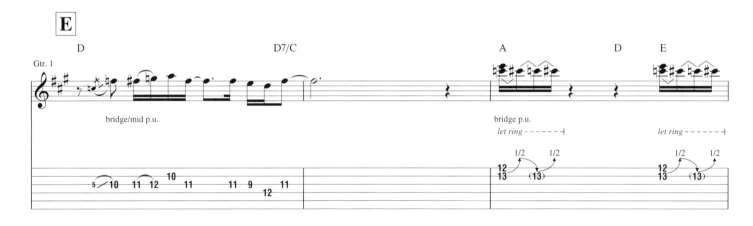

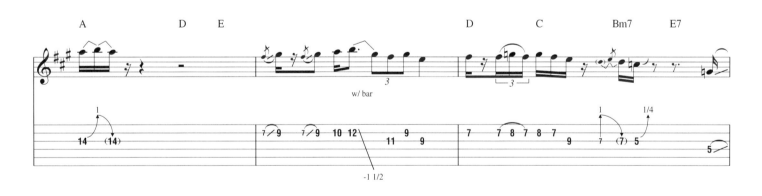

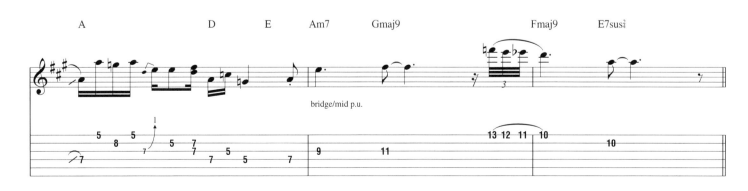

Constipated Duck

By Jeff Beck

*Chord symbols reflect implied harmony.

28

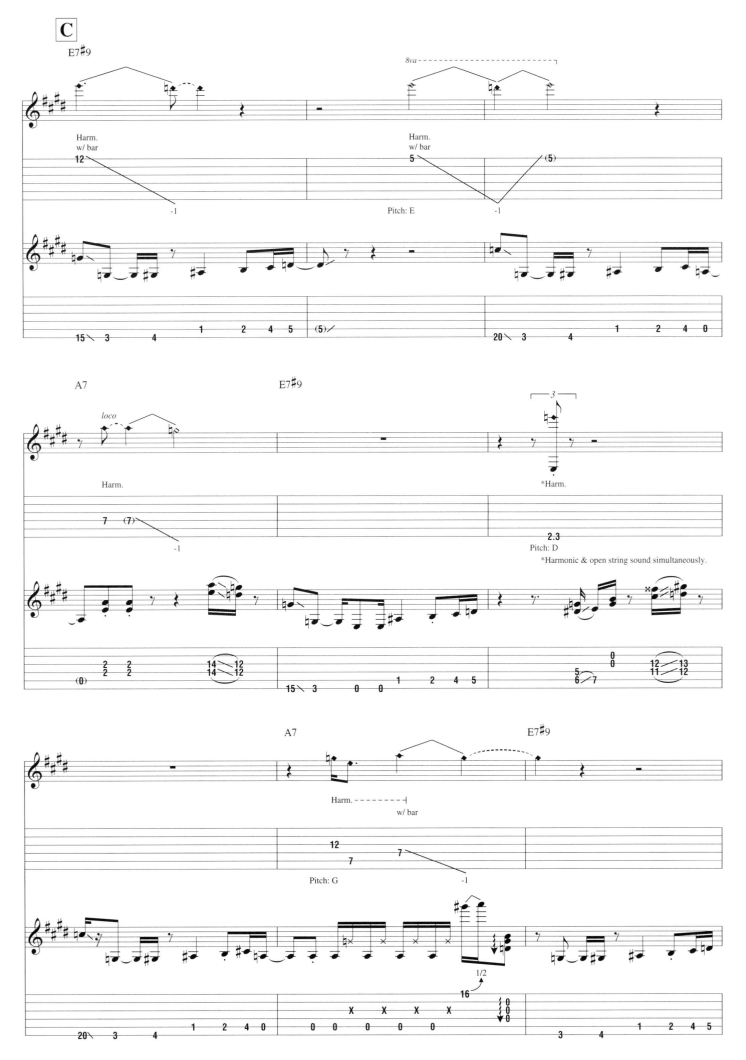

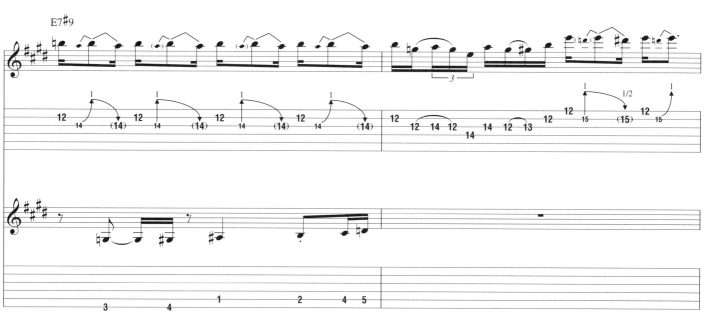

Air Blower

By Max Middleton, Jeff Beck, Philip Chenn and Richard Bailey

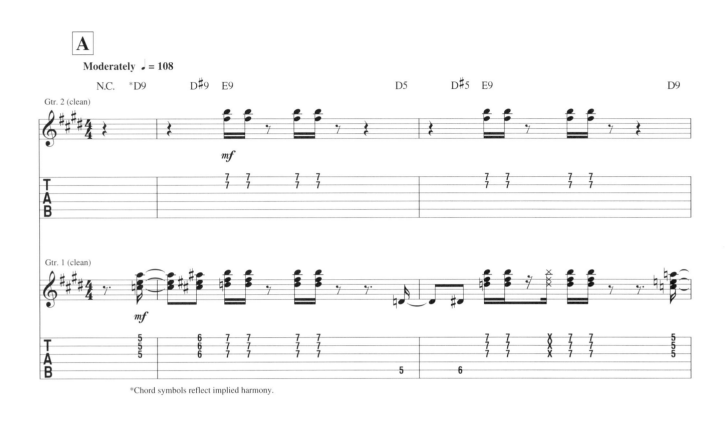

*Chord symbols reflect implied harmony.

*Synth. arr. for gtr.

**Chord symbols reflect overall harmony.

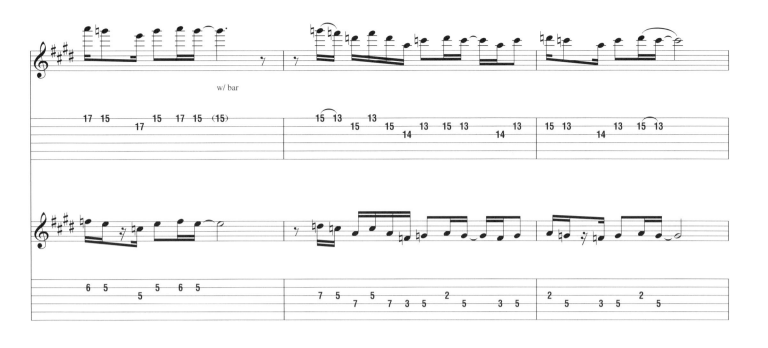

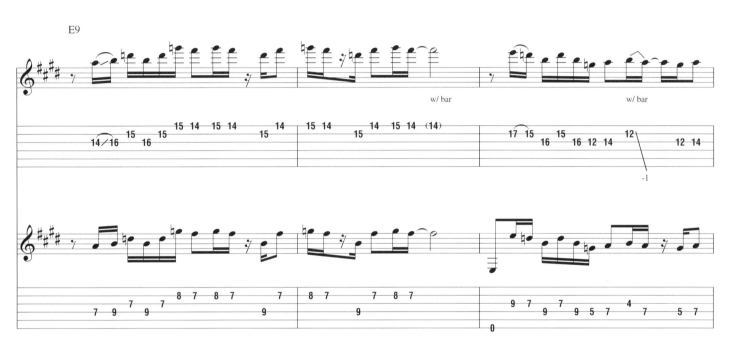

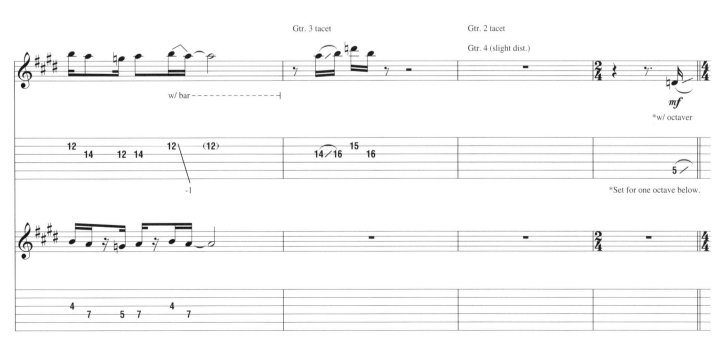

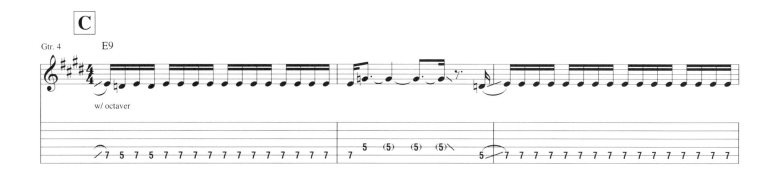

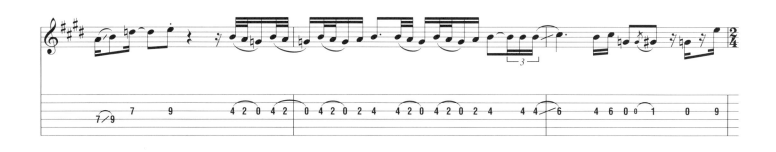

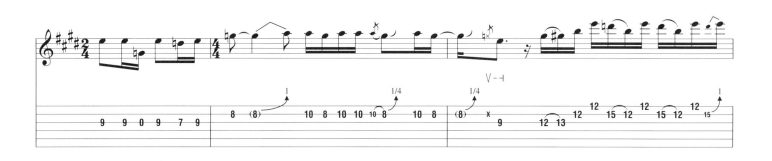

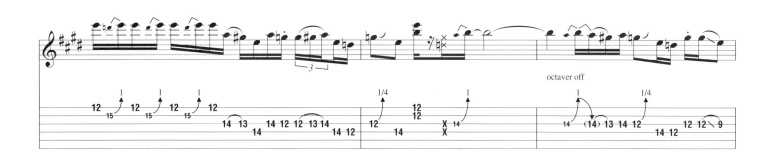

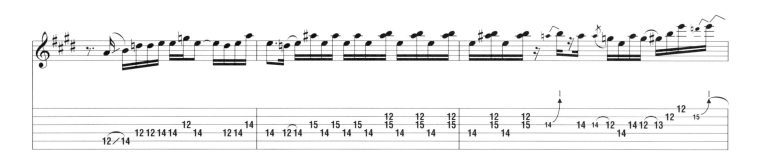

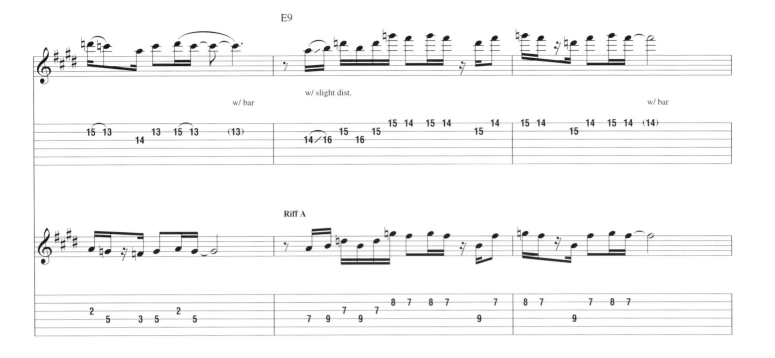

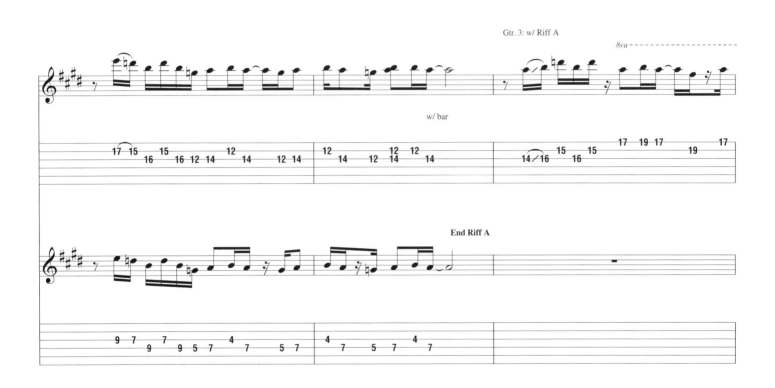

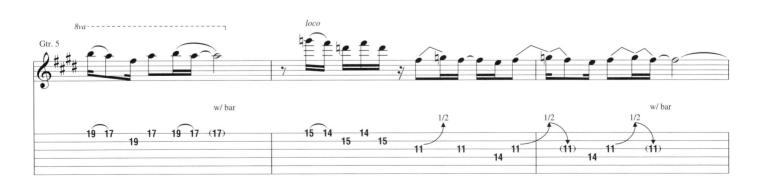

Gtr. 5 tacet

(11)

F

E7#9

*Gtr. 6

mf

*Elec. piano arr. for gtr.

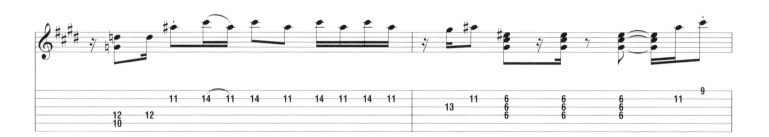

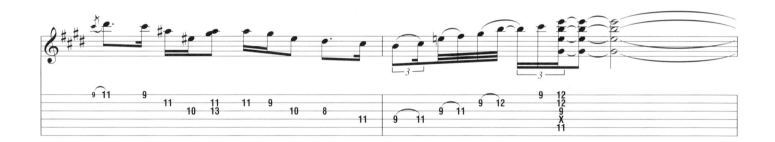

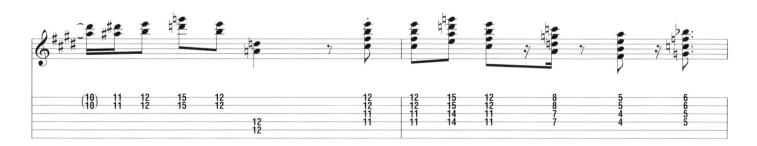

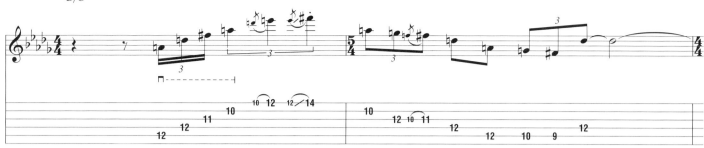

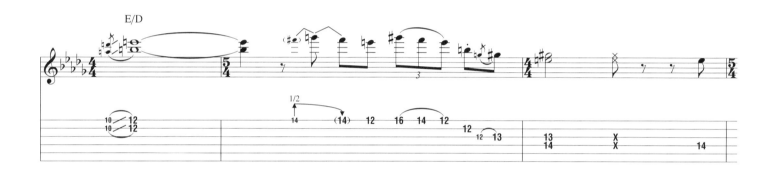

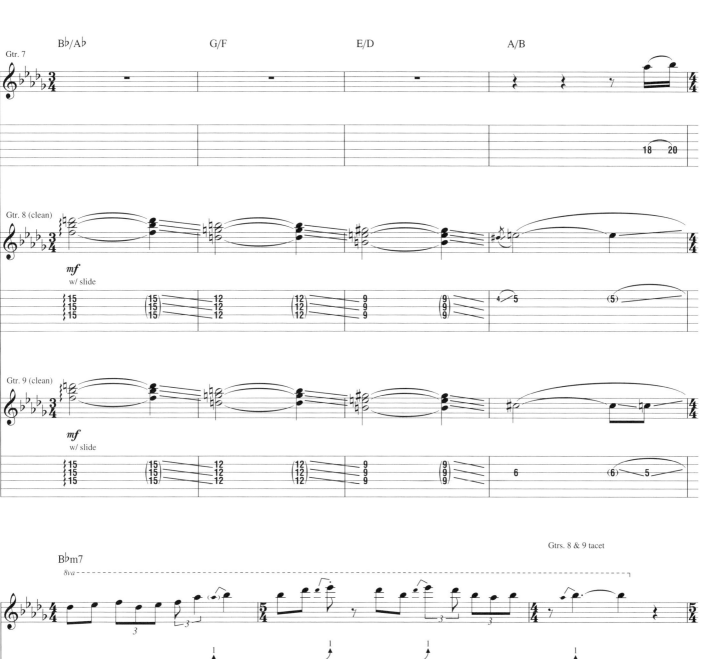

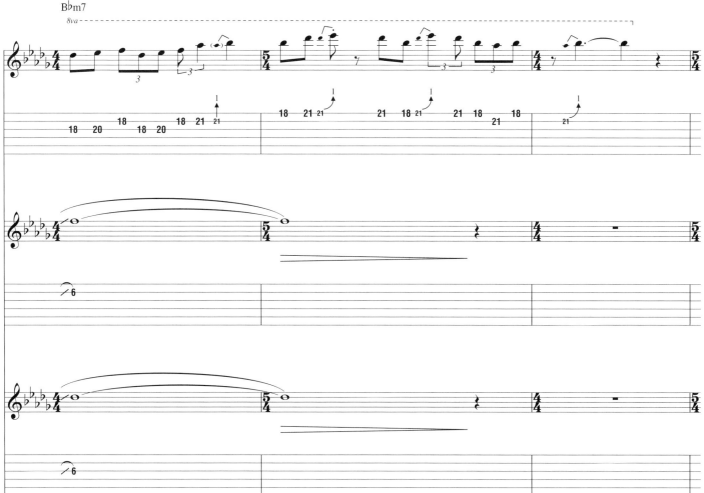

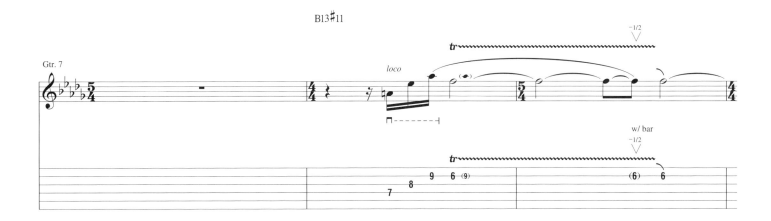

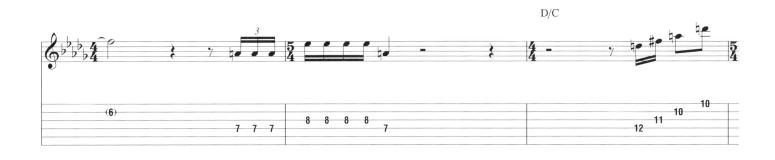

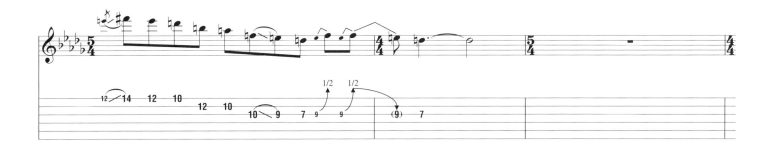

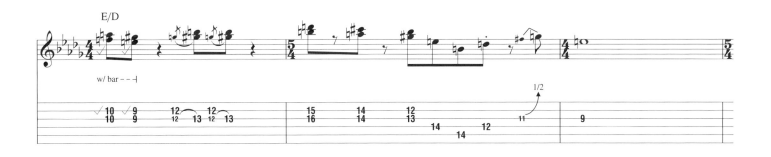

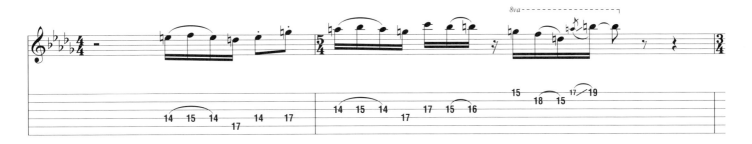

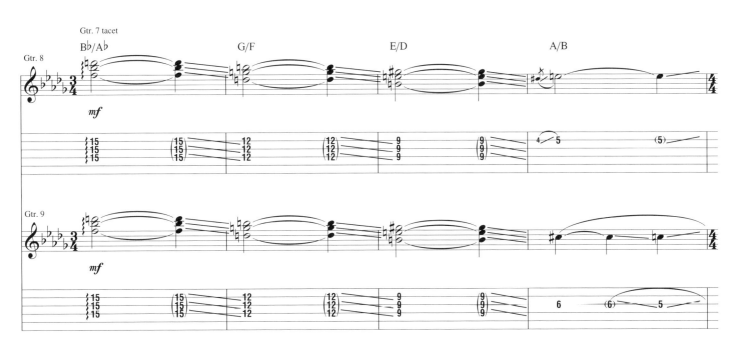

Free time

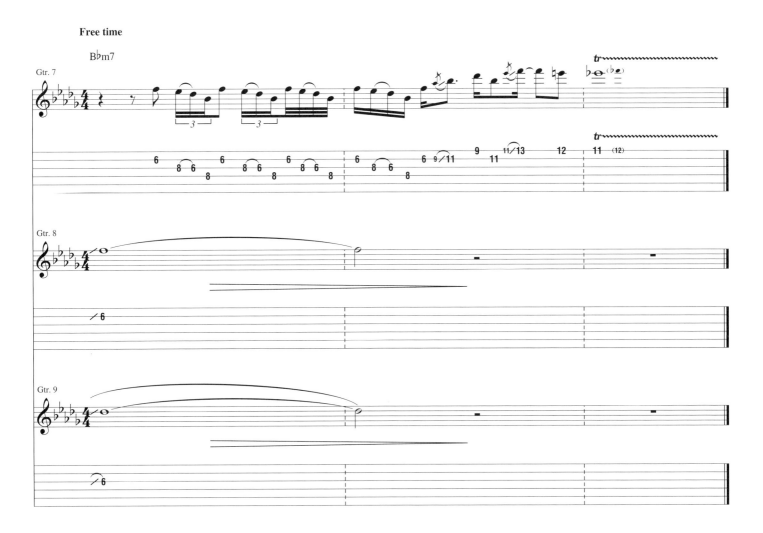

Scatterbrain

By Jeff Beck and Max Middleton

To Coda 1 ⊕

To Coda 2 ⊕

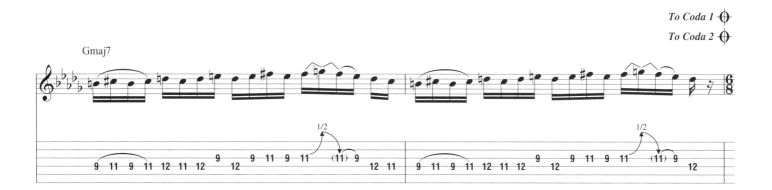

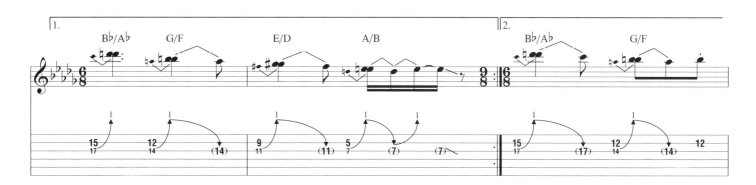

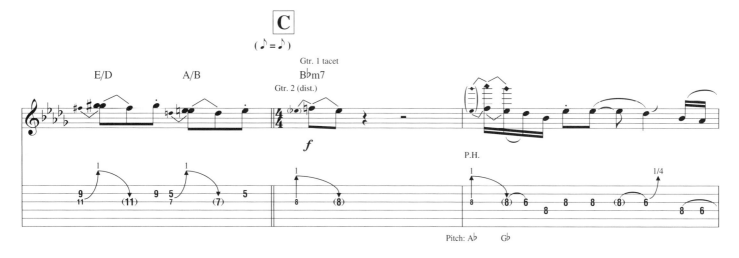

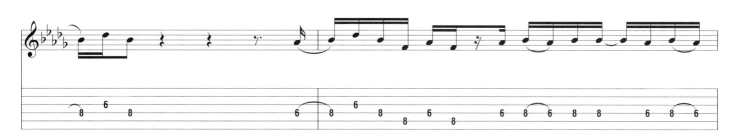

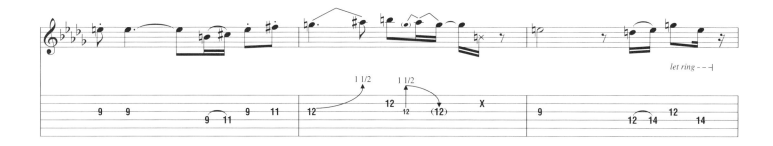

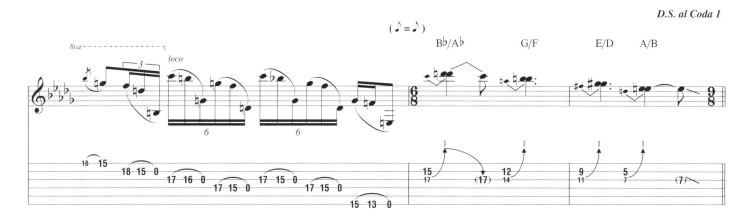

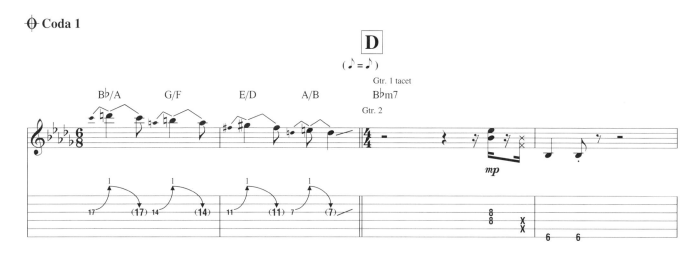

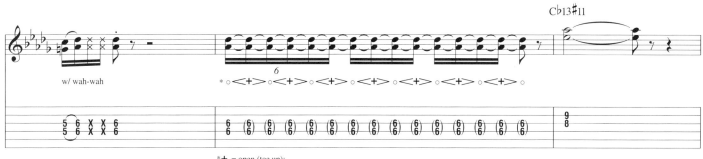

*+ = open (toe up);
○ = closed (toe down)

E/D

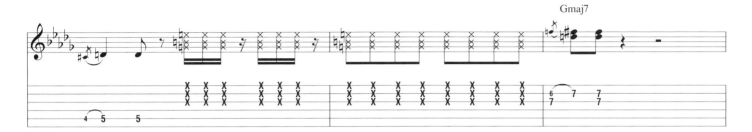

Gmaj7

D.S. al Coda 2

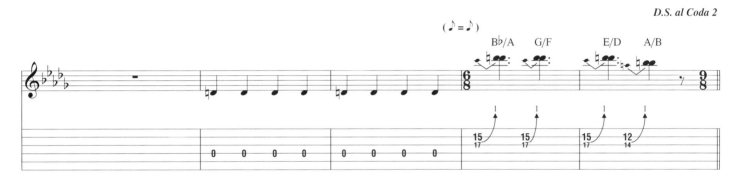

(♪ = ♪)

Bb/A   G/F   E/D   A/B

⊕ Coda 2

Free time
(♪ = ♪)

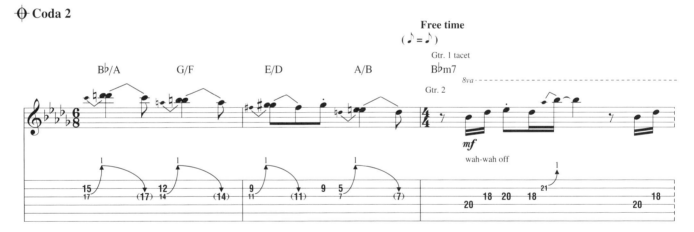

Bb/A   G/F   E/D   A/B   Gtr. 1 tacet
Bbm7

Gtr. 2

mf

wah-wah off

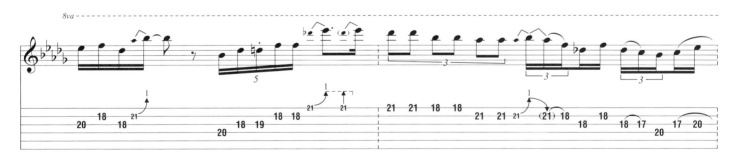

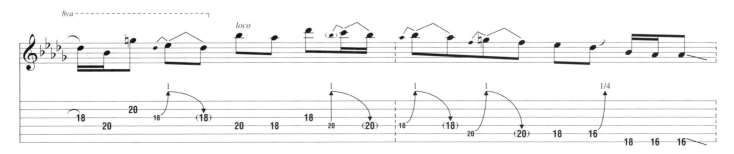

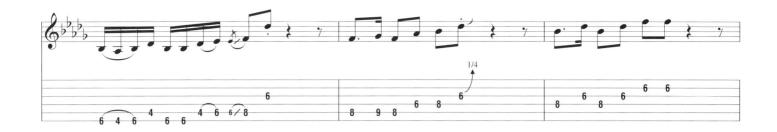

Begin fade

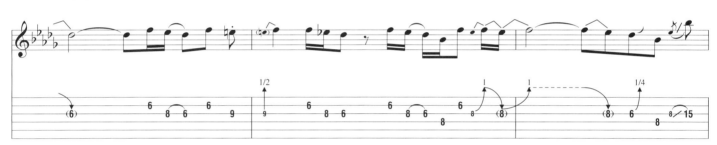

Fade out

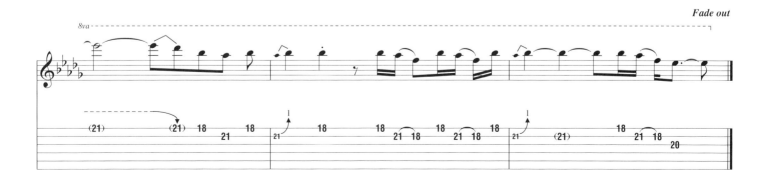

Cause We've Ended as Lovers

Words and Music by Stevie Wonder

*Chord symbols reflect overall harmony.
**Vol. swell
***Set for eighth-note regeneration w/ 1 repeat.

†Push down on string behind nut.

††Played w/ ring finger.

*Hammer onto note while manipulating vol. knob.

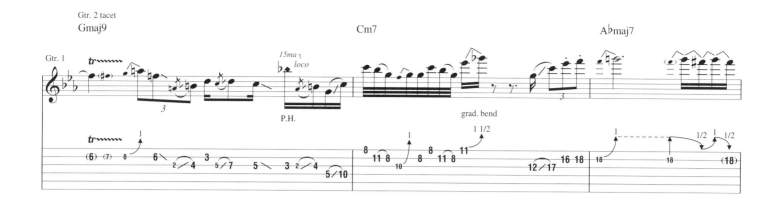

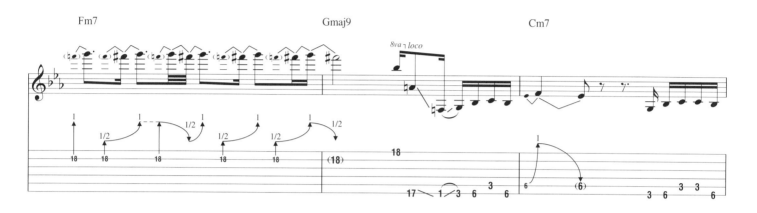

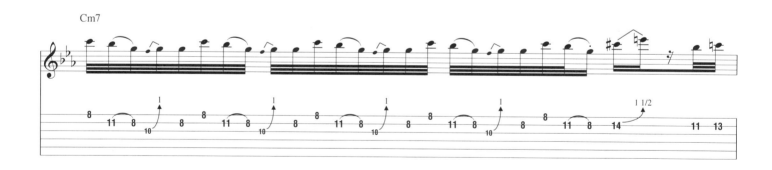

*Both strings caught and bent w/ ring finger.   **Played behind the beat.

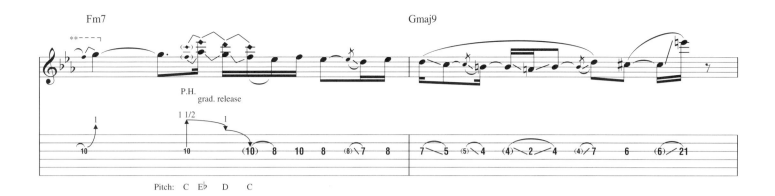

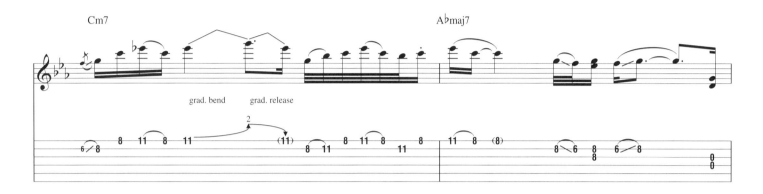

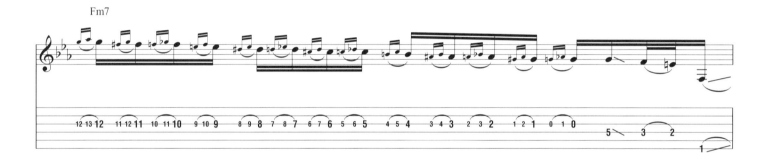

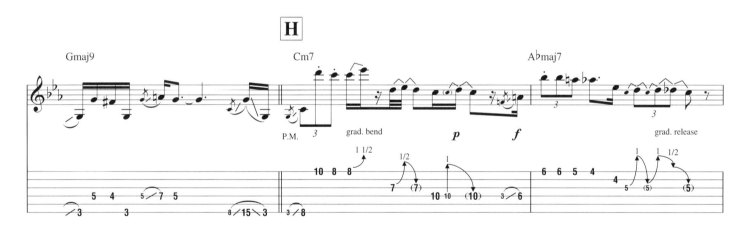

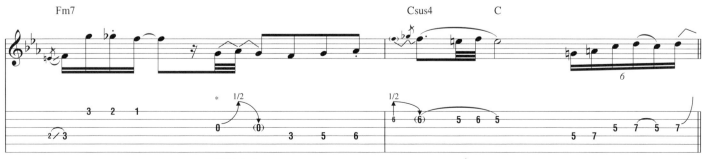

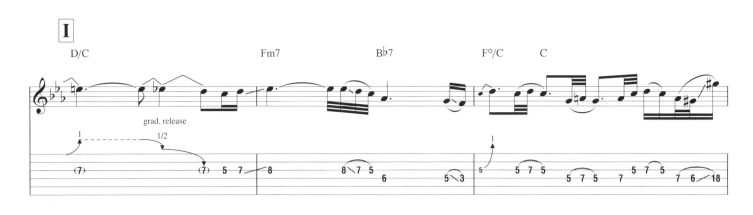

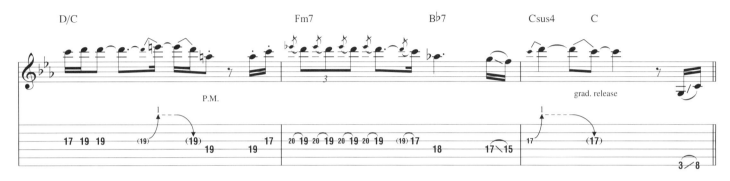

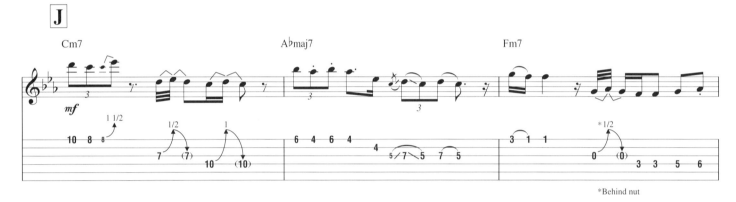

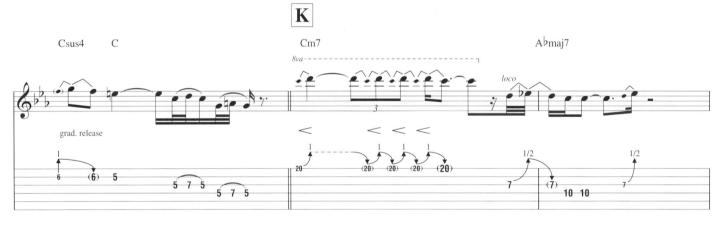

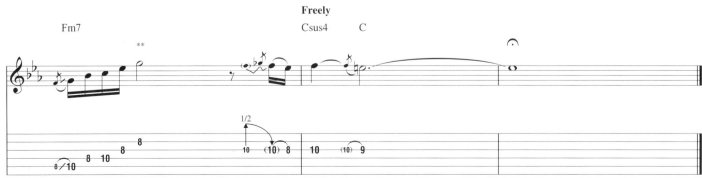

Thelonius

By Stevie Wonder

A

Moderately ♩ = 107

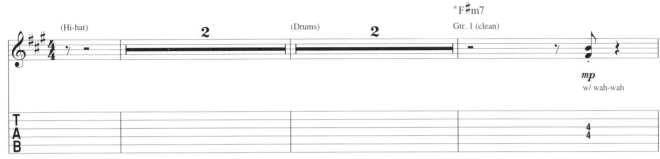

*Chord symbols reflect overall harmony.

Rhy. Fig. 1

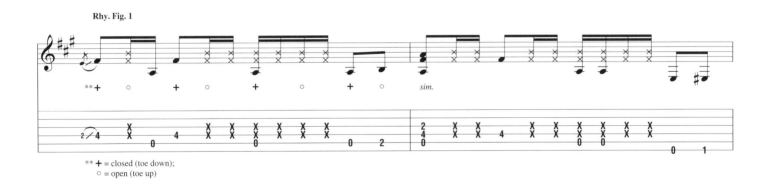

** + = closed (toe down);
○ = open (toe up)

End Rhy. Fig. 1

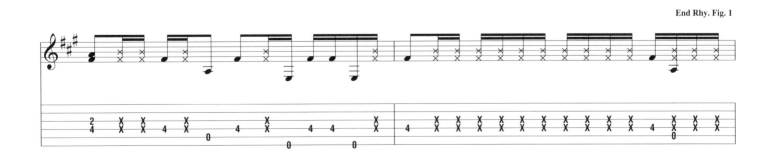

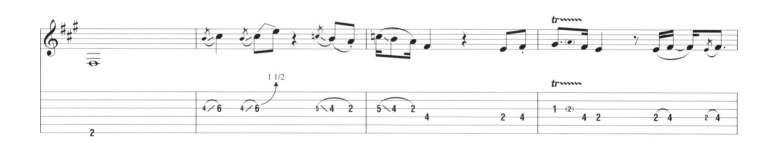

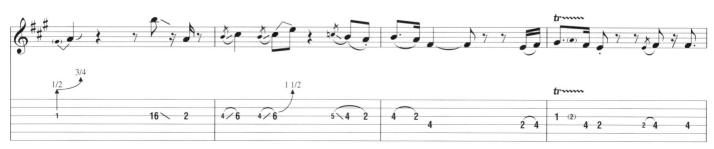

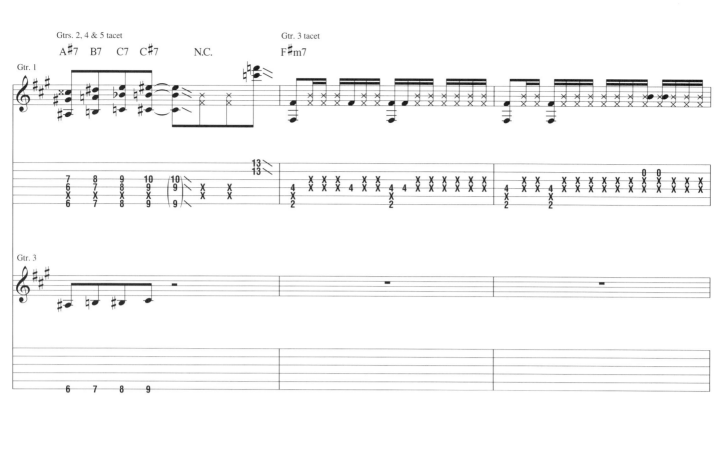

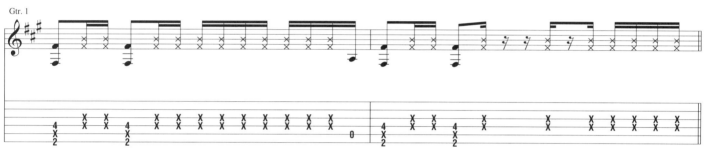

Gtr. 1: w/ Rhy. Fig. 1 (2 1/2 times)

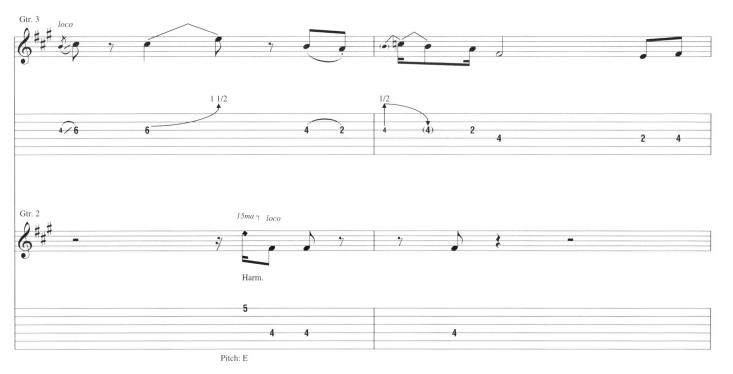

Pitch: E

Gtr. 2 tacet

Gtr. 3

Gtrs. 2, 4 & 5 tacet

Am7

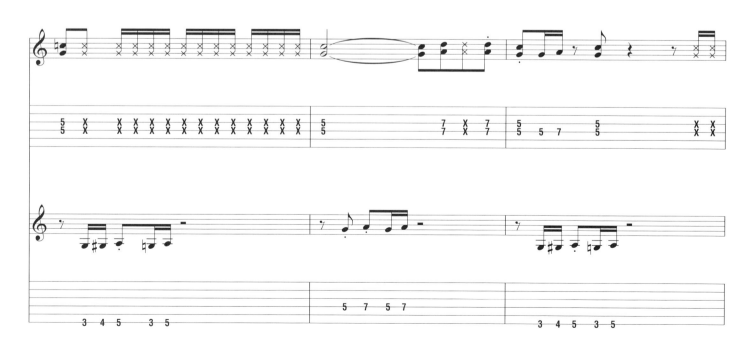

Begin fade

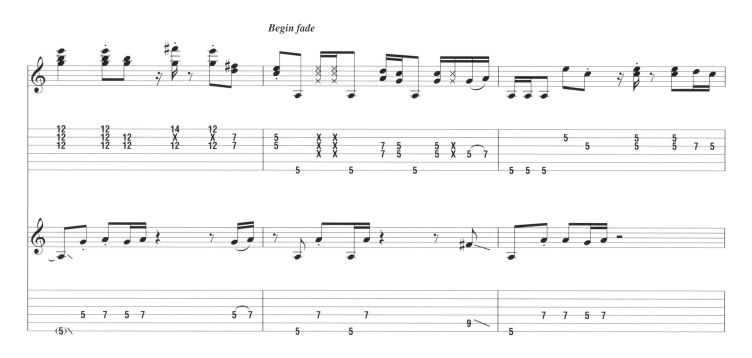

Segue to "Freeway Jam"
Fade out

Freeway Jam

By Max Middleton

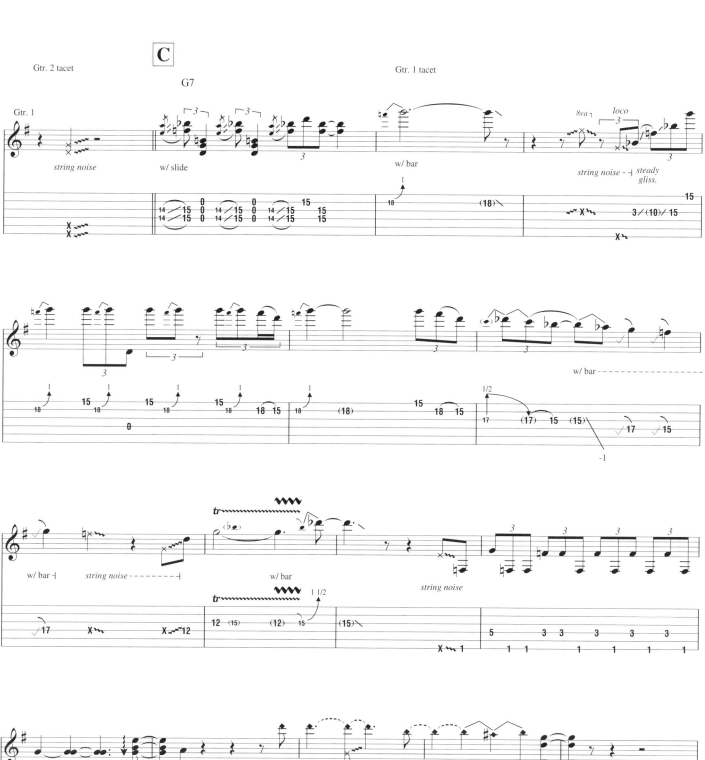

*③ is sounded symphathetically.

Pitch: D

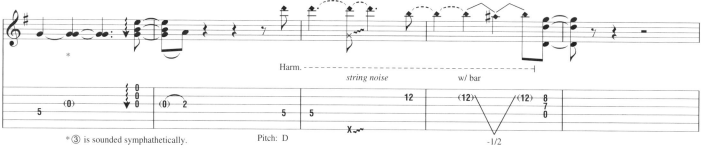

*Gtrs. 1 & 2

*Composite arrangement

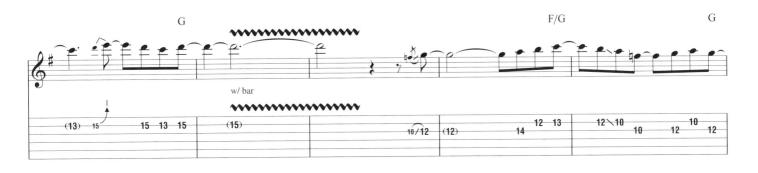

Gtr. 2: w/ Riff A (1 1/2 times)

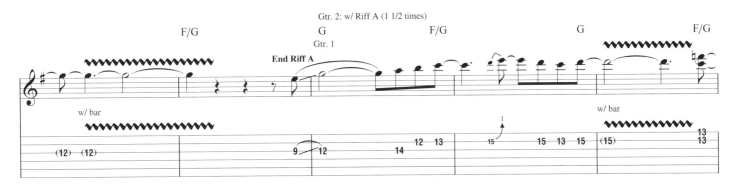

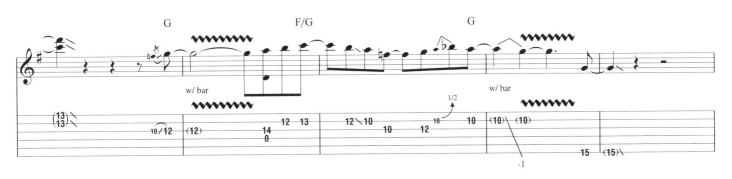

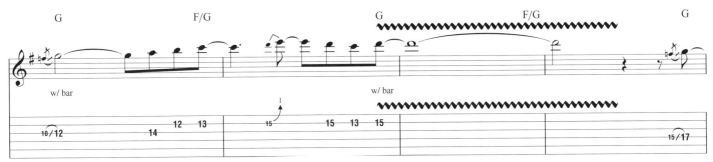

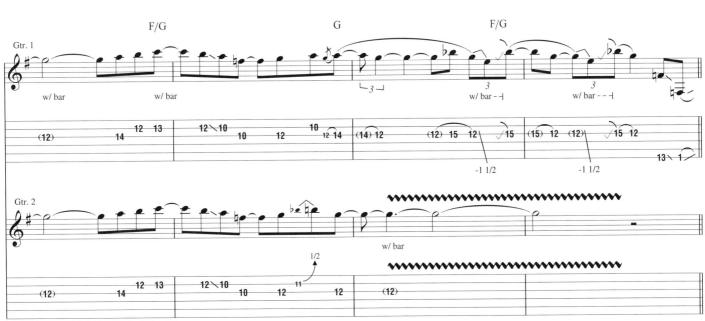

E

Gtr. 2 tacet

*Vol. swell

**Applies to P.H. only.

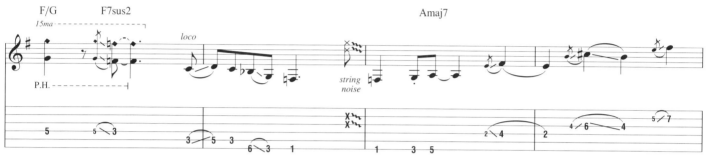

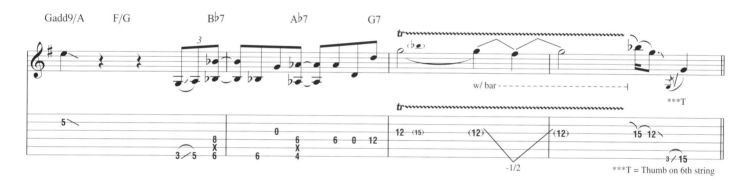

***T = Thumb on 6th string

F

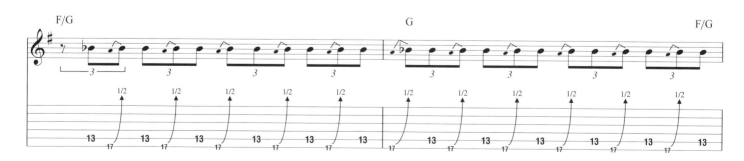

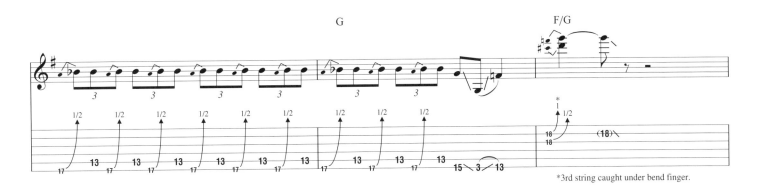

G   F/G

*3rd string caught under bend finger.

G   F/G   G   F/G

w/ bar
hold bend

string noise

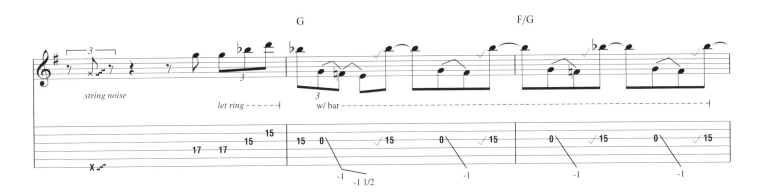

G   F/G

string noise
let ring
w/ bar

G

8va   loco

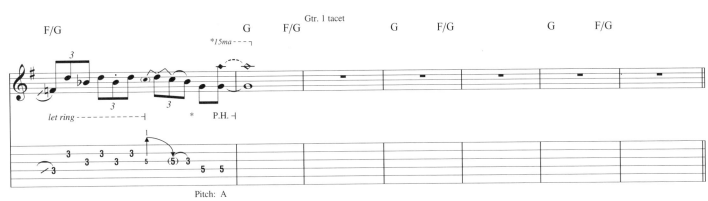

F/G   Gtr. 1 tacet   G   F/G   G   F/G   G   F/G

*15ma

let ring   *   P.H.

Pitch: A
*Applies to P.H. only.

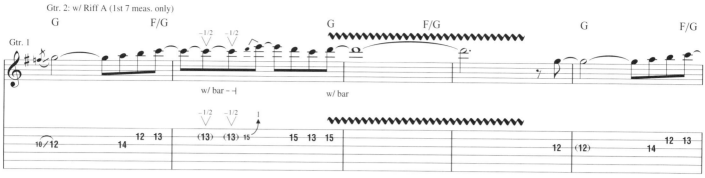

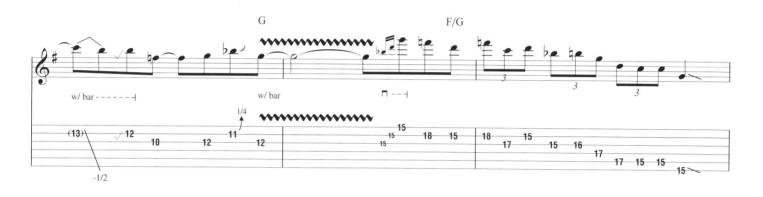

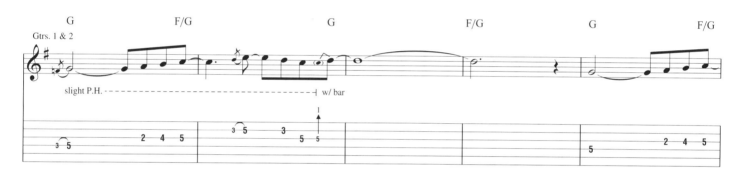

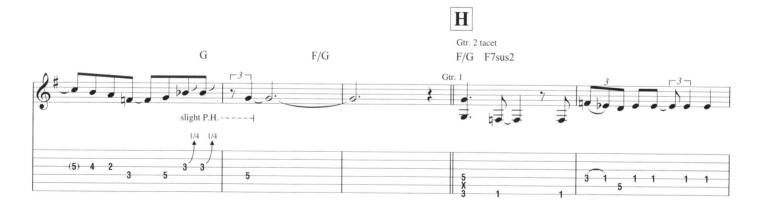

Diamond Dust

By Bernie Holland

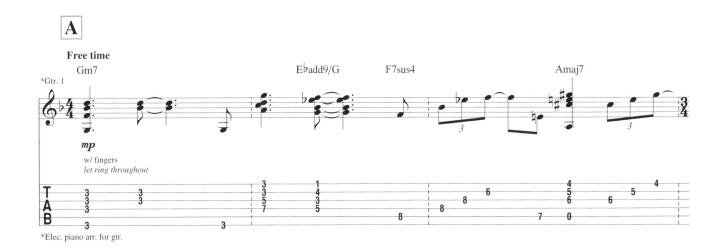

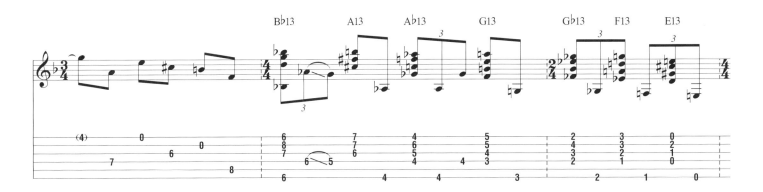

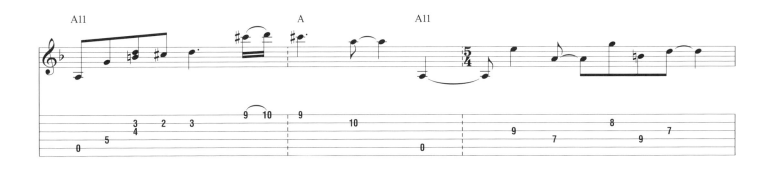

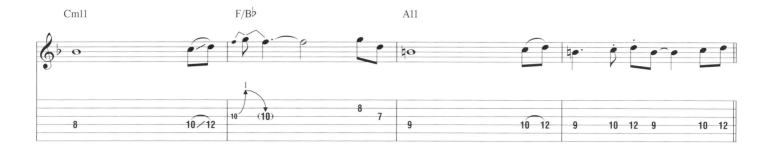

C

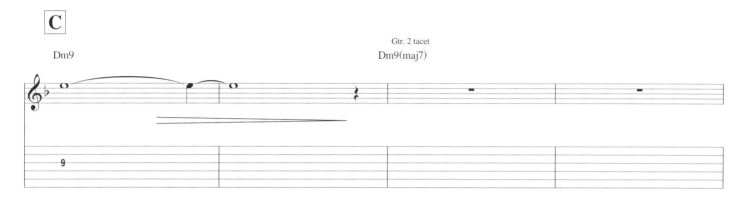

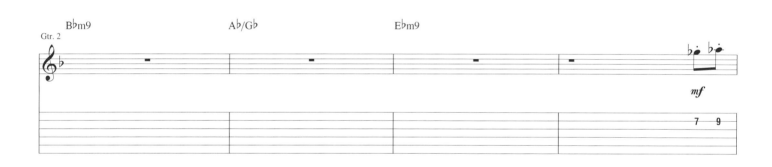

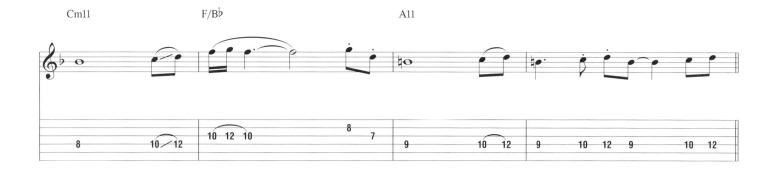

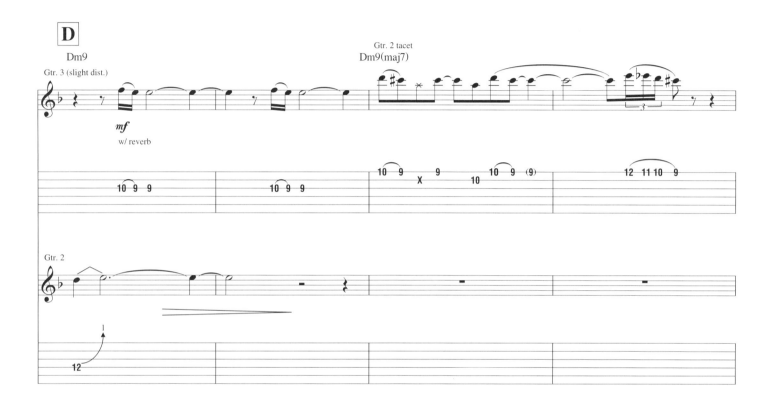

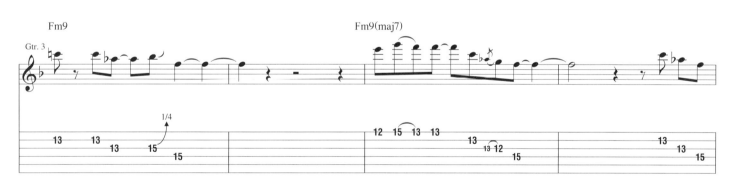

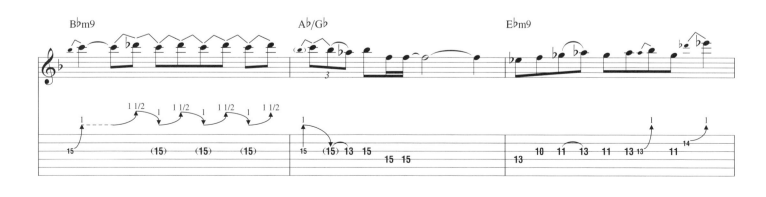

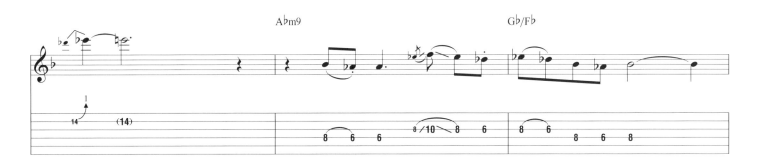

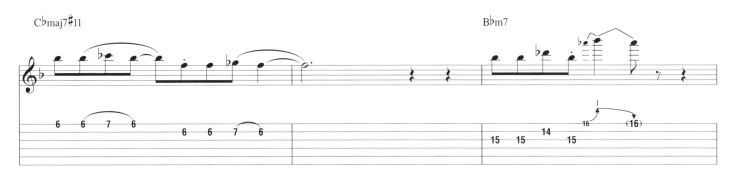

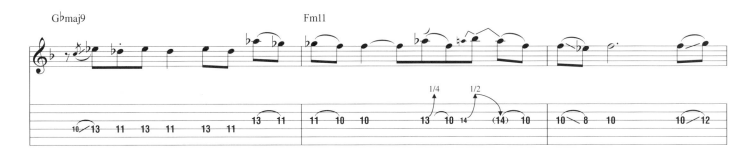

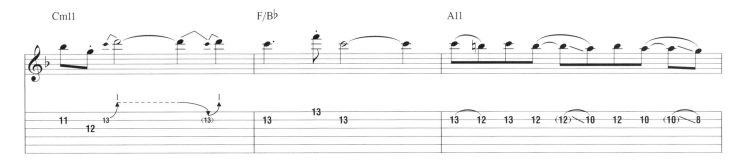

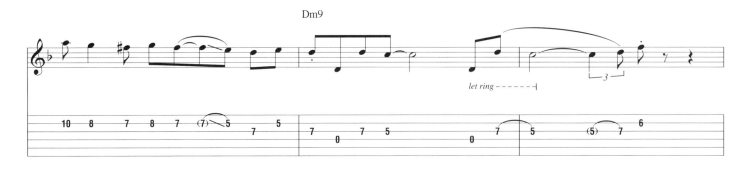

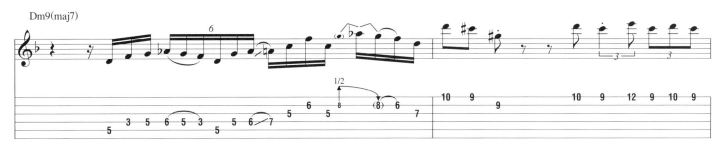

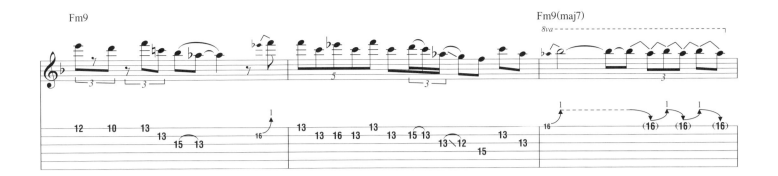

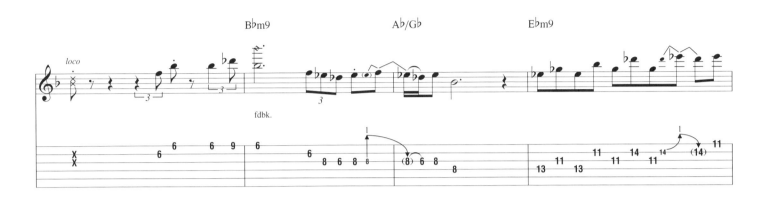

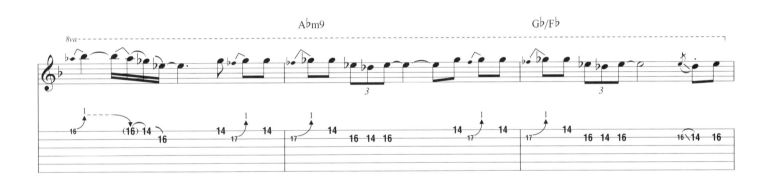

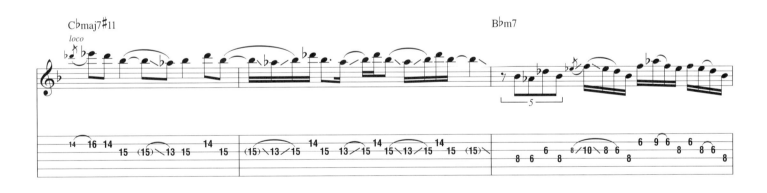

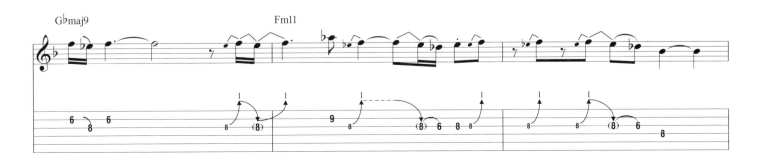

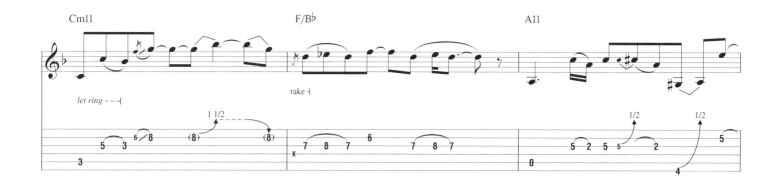

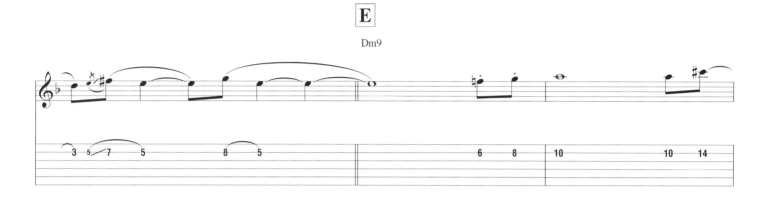

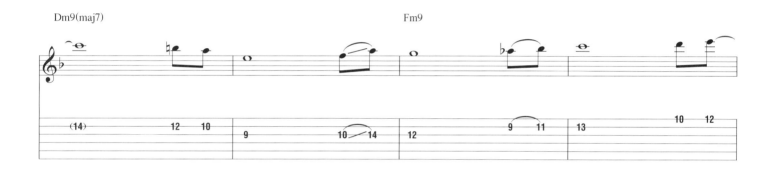

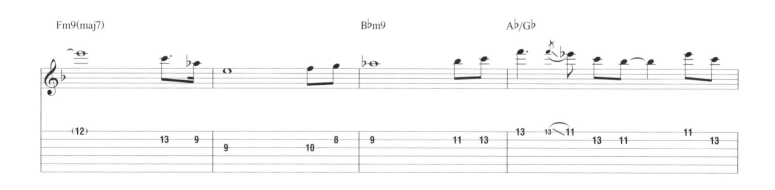

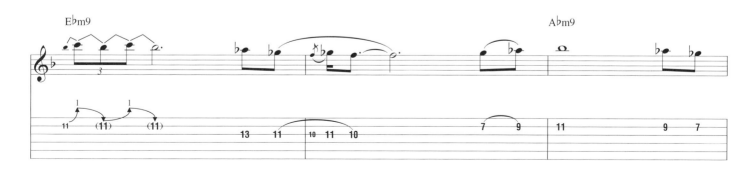

*Strings arr. for gtr.

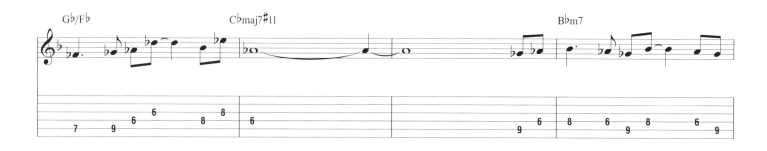

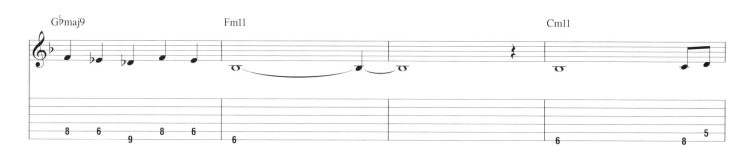

GUITAR NOTATION LEGEND

Guitar music can be notated three different ways: on a *musical staff*, in *tablature*, and in *rhythm slashes*.

RHYTHM SLASHES are written above the staff. Strum chords in the rhythm indicated. Use the chord diagrams found at the top of the first page of the transcription for the appropriate chord voicings. Round noteheads indicate single notes.

THE MUSICAL STAFF shows pitches and rhythms and is divided by bar lines into measures. Pitches are named after the first seven letters of the alphabet.

TABLATURE graphically represents the guitar fingerboard. Each horizontal line represents a string, and each number represents a fret.

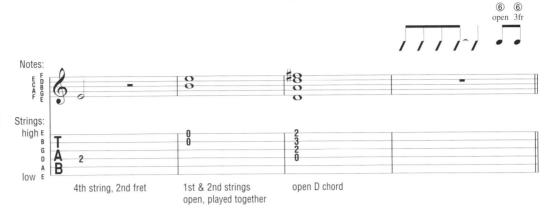

4th string, 2nd fret   1st & 2nd strings open, played together   open D chord

Definitions for Special Guitar Notation

HALF-STEP BEND: Strike the note and bend up 1/2 step.

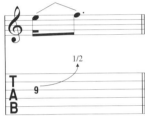

WHOLE-STEP BEND: Strike the note and bend up one step.

GRACE NOTE BEND: Strike the note and immediately bend up as indicated.

SLIGHT (MICROTONE) BEND: Strike the note and bend up 1/4 step.

BEND AND RELEASE: Strike the note and bend up as indicated, then release back to the original note. Only the first note is struck.

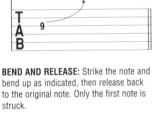

PRE-BEND: Bend the note as indicated, then strike it.

PRE-BEND AND RELEASE: Bend the note as indicated. Strike it and release the bend back to the original note.

UNISON BEND: Strike the two notes simultaneously and bend the lower note up to the pitch of the higher.

VIBRATO: The string is vibrated by rapidly bending and releasing the note with the fretting hand.

WIDE VIBRATO: The pitch is varied to a greater degree by vibrating with the fretting hand.

HAMMER-ON: Strike the first (lower) note with one finger, then sound the higher note (on the same string) with another finger by fretting it without picking.

PULL-OFF: Place both fingers on the notes to be sounded. Strike the first note and without picking, pull the finger off to sound the second (lower) note.

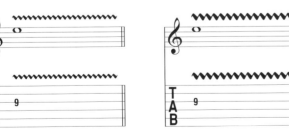

LEGATO SLIDE: Strike the first note and then slide the same fret-hand finger up or down to the second note. The second note is not struck.

SHIFT SLIDE: Same as legato slide, except the second note is struck.

TRILL: Very rapidly alternate between the notes indicated by continuously hammering on and pulling off.

TAPPING: Hammer ("tap") the fret indicated with the pick-hand index or middle finger and pull off to the note fretted by the fret hand.

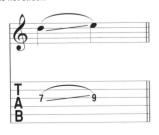

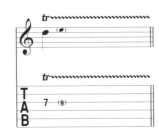

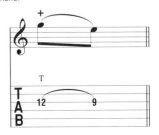

NATURAL HARMONIC: Strike the note while the fret-hand lightly touches the string directly over the fret indicated.

PINCH HARMONIC: The note is fretted normally and a harmonic is produced by adding the edge of the thumb or the tip of the index finger of the pick hand to the normal pick attack.

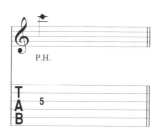

HARP HARMONIC: The note is fretted normally and a harmonic is produced by gently resting the pick hand's index finger directly above the indicated fret (in parentheses) while the pick hand's thumb or pick assists by plucking the appropriate string.

PICK SCRAPE: The edge of the pick is rubbed down (or up) the string, producing a scratchy sound.

MUFFLED STRINGS: A percussive sound is produced by laying the fret hand across the string(s) without depressing, and striking them with the pick hand.

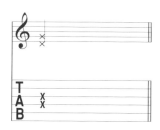

PALM MUTING: The note is partially muted by the pick hand lightly touching the string(s) just before the bridge.

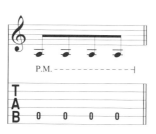

RAKE: Drag the pick across the strings indicated with a single motion.

TREMOLO PICKING: The note is picked as rapidly and continuously as possible.

ARPEGGIATE: Play the notes of the chord indicated by quickly rolling them from bottom to top.

VIBRATO BAR DIVE AND RETURN: The pitch of the note or chord is dropped a specified number of steps (in rhythm), then returned to the original pitch.

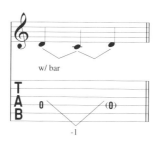

VIBRATO BAR SCOOP: Depress the bar just before striking the note, then quickly release the bar.

VIBRATO BAR DIP: Strike the note and then immediately drop a specified number of steps, then release back to the original pitch.

Additional Musical Definitions

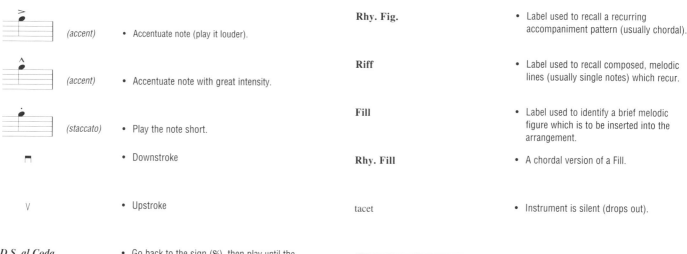

	(accent)	• Accentuate note (play it louder).
	(accent)	• Accentuate note with great intensity.
	(staccato)	• Play the note short.
◻		• Downstroke
V		• Upstroke
D.S. al Coda		• Go back to the sign (𝄋), then play until the measure marked "***To Coda***," then skip to the section labelled "**Coda**."
D.C. al Fine		• Go back to the beginning of the song and play until the measure marked "***Fine***" (end).

Rhy. Fig.	• Label used to recall a recurring accompaniment pattern (usually chordal).
Riff	• Label used to recall composed, melodic lines (usually single notes) which recur.
Fill	• Label used to identify a brief melodic figure which is to be inserted into the arrangement.
Rhy. Fill	• A chordal version of a Fill.
tacet	• Instrument is silent (drops out).
	• Repeat measures between signs.
	• When a repeated section has different endings, play the first ending only the first time and the second ending only the second time.

NOTE: Tablature numbers in parentheses mean:
1. The note is being sustained over a system (note in standard notation is tied), or
2. The note is sustained, but a new articulation (such as a hammer-on, pull-off, slide or vibrato) begins, or
3. The note is a barely audible "ghost" note (note in standard notation is also in parentheses).

GUITAR *signature licks*

Signature Licks book/CD packs provide a step-by-step breakdown of "right from the record" riffs, licks, and solos so you can jam along with your favorite bands. They contain performance notes and an overview of each artist's or group's style, with note-for-note transcriptions in notes and tab. The CDs feature full-band demos at both normal and slow speeds.

ACOUSTIC CLASSICS
00695864 ....$19.95

AEROSMITH 1973-1979
00695106 ....$22.95

AEROSMITH 1979-1998
00695219 ....$22.95

BEST OF AGGRO-METAL
00695592 ....$19.95

DUANE ALLMAN
00696042 ....$22.95

BEST OF CHET ATKINS
00695752 ....$22.95

THE BEACH BOYS DEFINITIVE COLLECTION
00695683 ....$22.95

BEST OF THE BEATLES FOR ACOUSTIC GUITAR
00695453 ....$22.95

THE BEATLES BASS
00695283 ....$22.95

THE BEATLES FAVORITES
00695096 ....$24.95

THE BEATLES HITS
00695049 ....$24.95

BEST OF GEORGE BENSON
00695418 ....$22.95

BEST OF BLACK SABBATH
00695249 ....$22.95

BEST OF BLINK - 182
00695704 ....$22.95

BEST OF BLUES GUITAR
00695846 ....$19.95

BLUES GUITAR CLASSICS
00695177 ....$19.95

BLUES/ROCK GUITAR MASTERS
00695348 ....$21.95

KENNY BURRELL
00695830 ....$22.99

BEST OF CHARLIE CHRISTIAN
00695584 ....$22.95

BEST OF ERIC CLAPTON
00695038 ....$24.95

ERIC CLAPTON – THE BLUESMAN
00695040 ....$22.95

ERIC CLAPTON – FROM THE ALBUM UNPLUGGED
00695250 ....$24.95

BEST OF CREAM
00695251 ....$22.95

CREEDANCE CLEARWATER REVIVAL
00695924 ....$22.95

DEEP PURPLE – GREATEST HITS
00695625 ....$22.95

THE BEST OF DEF LEPPARD
00696516 ....$22.95

THE DOORS
00695373 ....$22.95

ESSENTIAL JAZZ GUITAR
00695875 ....$19.99

FAMOUS ROCK GUITAR SOLOS
00695590 ....$19.95

BEST OF FOO FIGHTERS
00695481 ....$24.95

ROBBEN FORD
00695903 ....$22.95

GREATEST GUITAR SOLOS OF ALL TIME
00695301 ....$19.95

BEST OF GRANT GREEN
00695747 ....$22.95

BEST OF GUNS N' ROSES
00695183 ....$24.95

THE BEST OF BUDDY GUY
00695186 ....$22.95

JIM HALL
00695848 ....$22.99

HARD ROCK SOLOS
00695591 ....$19.95

JIMI HENDRIX
00696560 ....$24.95

JIMI HENDRIX – VOLUME 2
00695835 ....$24.95

JOHN LEE HOOKER
00695894 ....$19.99

HOT COUNTRY GUITAR
00695580 ....$19.95

BEST OF JAZZ GUITAR
00695586 ....$24.95

ERIC JOHNSON
00699317 ....$24.95

ROBERT JOHNSON
00695264 ....$22.95

BARNEY KESSEL
00696009 ....$22.99

THE ESSENTIAL ALBERT KING
00695713 ....$22.95

B.B. KING – THE DEFINITIVE COLLECTION
00695635 ....$22.95

B.B. KING – MASTER BLUESMAN
00699923 ....$24.99

THE KINKS
00695553 ....$22.95

BEST OF KISS
00699413 ....$22.95

MARK KNOPFLER
00695178 ....$22.95

LYNYRD SKYNYRD
00695872 ....$24.95

BEST OF YNGWIE MALMSTEEN
00695669 ....$22.95

BEST OF PAT MARTINO
00695632 ....$24.99

WES MONTGOMERY
00695387 ....$24.95

BEST OF NIRVANA
00695483 ....$24.95

THE OFFSPRING
00695852 ....$24.95

VERY BEST OF OZZY OSBOURNE
00695431 ....$22.95

BEST OF JOE PASS
00695730 ....$22.95

TOM PETTY
00696021 ....$22.99

PINK FLOYD – EARLY CLASSICS
00695566 ....$22.95

THE POLICE
00695724 ....$22.95

THE GUITARS OF ELVIS
00696507 ....$22.95

BEST OF QUEEN
00695097 ....$24.95

BEST OF RAGE AGAINST THE MACHINE
00695480 ....$24.95

RED HOT CHILI PEPPERS
00695173 ....$22.95

RED HOT CHILI PEPPERS – GREATEST HITS
00695828 ....$24.95

BEST OF DJANGO REINHARDT
00695660 ....$24.95

BEST OF ROCK
00695884 ....$19.95

BEST OF ROCK 'N' ROLL GUITAR
00695559 ....$19.95

BEST OF ROCKABILLY GUITAR
00695785 ....$19.95

THE ROLLING STONES
00695079 ....$24.95

BEST OF DAVID LEE ROTH
00695843 ....$24.95

BEST OF JOE SATRIANI
00695216 ....$22.95

BEST OF SILVERCHAIR
00695488 ....$22.95

THE BEST OF SOUL GUITAR
00695703 ....$19.95

BEST OF SOUTHERN ROCK
00695560 ....$19.95

MIKE STERN
00695800 ....$24.99

ROD STEWART
00695663 ....$22.95

BEST OF SURF GUITAR
00695822 ....$19.95

BEST OF SYSTEM OF A DOWN
00695788 ....$22.95

ROCK BAND
00696063 ....$22.99

ROBIN TROWER
00695950 ....$22.95

STEVE VAI
00673247 ....$22.95

STEVE VAI – ALIEN LOVE SECRETS: THE NAKED VAMPS
00695223 ....$22.95

STEVE VAI – FIRE GARDEN: THE NAKED VAMPS
00695166 ....$22.95

STEVE VAI – THE ULTRA ZONE: NAKED VAMPS
00695684 ....$22.95

STEVIE RAY VAUGHAN – 2ND ED.
00699316 ....$24.95

THE GUITAR STYLE OF STEVIE RAY VAUGHAN
00695155 ....$24.95

BEST OF THE VENTURES
00695772 ....$19.95

THE WHO – 2ND ED.
00695561 ....$22.95

JOHNNY WINTER
00695951 ....$22.99

BEST OF ZZ TOP
00695738 ....$24.95

FOR MORE INFORMATION,
SEE YOUR LOCAL MUSIC DEALER,
OR WRITE TO:

HAL•LEONARD® CORPORATION
7777 W. BLUEMOUND RD. P.O. BOX 13819
MILWAUKEE, WISCONSIN 53213

www.halleonard.com

COMPLETE DESCRIPTIONS AND SONGLISTS ONLINE!
Prices, contents and availability subject to change without notice.

0410

GUITAR RECORDED VERSIONS®

AUTHENTIC TRANSCRIPTIONS WITH NOTES AND TABLATURE

Guitar Recorded Versions® are note-for-note transcriptions of guitar music taken directly off recordings. This series, one of the most popular in print today, features some of the greatest guitar players and groups from blues and rock to country and jazz.

Guitar Recorded Versions are transcribed by the best transcribers in the business. Every book contains notes and tablature. Visit www.halleonard.com for our complete selection.

00690016 The Will Ackerman Collection $19.95
00690501 Bryan Adams – Greatest Hits $19.95
00690002 Aerosmith – Big Ones $24.95
00692015 Aerosmith – Greatest Hits $22.95
00690603 Aerosmith – O Yeah! (Ultimate Hits) $24.95
00690147 Aerosmith – Rocks $19.95
00690146 Aerosmith – Toys in the Attic $19.99
00690139 Alice in Chains $19.95
00690178 Alice in Chains – Acoustic $19.95
00694865 Alice in Chains – Dirt $19.95
00660225 Alice in Chains – Facelift $19.95
00694925 Alice in Chains – Jar of Flies/Sap $19.95
00690387 Alice in Chains – Nothing Safe: Best of the Box $19.95
00690899 All That Remains – The Fall of Ideals $19.95
00690980 All That Remains – Overcome $22.99
00690812 All-American Rejects – Move Along $19.95
00690983 All-American Rejects – When the World Comes Down $22.99
00694932 Allman Brothers Band – Definitive Collection for Guitar Volume 1 ....$24.95
00694933 Allman Brothers Band – Definitive Collection for Guitar Volume 2 ....$24.95
00694934 Allman Brothers Band – Definitive Collection for Guitar Volume 3 ....$24.95
00690958 Duane Allman Guitar Anthology $24.99
00690945 Alter Bridge – Blackbird $22.99
00690755 Alter Bridge – One Day Remains $19.95
00690571 Trey Anastasio $19.95
00691013 The Answer – Everyday Demons $19.99
00690158 Chet Atkins – Almost Alone $19.95
00694876 Chet Atkins – Contemporary Styles $19.95
00694878 Chet Atkins – Vintage Fingerstyle $19.95
00690865 Atreyu – A Deathgrip on Yesterday $19.95
00690609 Audioslave $19.95
00690804 Audioslave – Out of Exile $19.95
00690884 Audioslave – Revelations $19.95
00690926 Avenged Sevenfold $22.95
00690820 Avenged Sevenfold – City of Evil $24.95
00694918 Randy Bachman Collection $22.95
00690366 Bad Company – Original Anthology – Book 1 ....$19.95
00690367 Bad Company – Original Anthology – Book 2 ....$19.95
00690503 Beach Boys – Very Best of $19.95
00694929 Beatles: 1962-1966 ....$24.95
00694930 Beatles: 1967-1970 ....$24.95
00690489 Beatles – 1 ....$24.99
00694880 Beatles – Abbey Road $19.95
00690110 Beatles – Book 1 (White Album) $19.95
00690111 Beatles – Book 2 (White Album) $19.95
00690902 Beatles – The Capitol Albums, Volume 1 ....$24.99
00694832 Beatles – For Acoustic Guitar $22.99
00690137 Beatles – A Hard Day's Night $16.95
00691031 Beatles – Help! $19.99
00690482 Beatles – Let It Be $17.95
00694891 Beatles – Revolver $19.95
00694914 Beatles – Rubber Soul $19.95
00694863 Beatles – Sgt. Pepper's Lonely Hearts Club Band $19.95
00690383 Beatles – Yellow Submarine $19.95
00690632 Beck – Sea Change $19.95
00694884 Best of George Benson $19.95
00692385 Chuck Berry $19.95
00690835 Billy Talent $19.95
00690879 Billy Talent II $19.95
00690149 Black Sabbath $14.95
00690901 Best of Black Sabbath $19.95
00691010 Black Sabbath – Heaven and Hell $22.99
00690148 Black Sabbath – Master of Reality $14.95
00690142 Black Sabbath – Paranoid $14.95
00692200 Black Sabbath – We Sold Our Soul for Rock 'N' Roll $19.95
00690674 blink-182 ....$19.95
00690389 blink-182 – Enema of the State $19.95
00690831 blink-182 – Greatest Hits $19.95
00690523 blink-182 – Take Off Your Pants and Jacket $19.95
00690028 Blue Oyster Cult – Cult Classics $19.95
00690851 James Blunt – Back to Bedlam $22.95
00690008 Bon Jovi – Cross Road $19.95
00690827 Bon Jovi – Have a Nice Day $22.95
00690913 Boston $19.95
00690932 Boston – Don't Look Back $19.99
00690829 Boston Guitar Collection $19.99
00690491 Best of David Bowie $19.95
00690583 Box Car Racer $19.95
00691023 Breaking Benjamin – Dear Agony $22.99
00690873 Breaking Benjamin – Phobia $19.95
00690764 Breaking Benjamin – We Are Not Alone $19.95
00690451 Jeff Buckley Collection $24.95
00690957 Bullet for My Valentine – Scream Aim Fire $19.95
00690678 Best of Kenny Burrell $19.95
00690564 The Calling – Camino Palmero $19.95
00690261 Carter Family Collection $19.95
00690043 Best of Cheap Trick $19.95
00690171 Chicago – The Definitive Guitar Collection $22.95
00691004 Chickenfoot $22.99
00691011 Chimaira Guitar Collection $24.99
00690567 Charlie Christian – The Definitive Collection $19.95
00690590 Eric Clapton – Anthology $29.95
00692391 Best of Eric Clapton – 2nd Edition $22.95
00690936 Eric Clapton – Complete Clapton $29.99
00690074 Eric Clapton – Cream of Clapton $24.95
00690247 Eric Clapton – 461 Ocean Boulevard $19.99
00690010 Eric Clapton – From the Cradle $19.95
00690716 Eric Clapton – Me and Mr. Johnson $19.95
00694873 Eric Clapton – Timepieces $19.95
00694869 Eric Clapton – Unplugged $22.95
00690415 Clapton Chronicles – Best of Eric Clapton $18.95
00694896 John Mayall/Eric Clapton – Bluesbreakers $19.95
00690162 Best of the Clash $19.95
00690828 Coheed & Cambria – Good Apollo I'm Burning Star, IV, Vol. 1: From Fear Through the Eyes of Madness $19.95
00690940 Coheed and Cambria – No World for Tomorrow $19.95
00690494 Coldplay – Parachutes $19.95
00690593 Coldplay – A Rush of Blood to the Head $19.95
00690906 Coldplay – The Singles & B-Sides $24.95
00690962 Coldplay – Viva La Vida $19.95
00690806 Coldplay – X & Y $19.95
00690855 Best of Collective Soul $19.95
00690928 Chris Cornell – Carry On $19.95
00694940 Counting Crows – August & Everything After $19.95
00690405 Counting Crows – This Desert Life $19.95
00694840 Cream – Disraeli Gears $19.95
00690285 Cream – Those Were the Days $17.95
00690819 Best of Creedence Clearwater Revival $22.95
00690648 The Very Best of Jim Croce $19.95
00690572 Steve Cropper – Soul Man $19.95
00690613 Best of Crosby, Stills & Nash $22.95
00690777 Crossfade $19.95
00699521 The Cure – Greatest Hits $24.95
00690637 Best of Dick Dale $19.95
00690941 Dashboard Confessional – The Shade of Poison Trees $19.95
00690892 Daughtry $19.95
00690822 Best of Alex De Grassi $19.95
00690967 Death Cab for Cutie – Narrow Stairs $22.99
00690289 Best of Deep Purple $17.95
00690288 Deep Purple – Machine Head $17.99
00690784 Best of Def Leppard $19.95
00694831 Derek and the Dominos – Layla & Other Assorted Love Songs $22.95
00692240 Bo Diddley – Guitar Solos by Fred Sokolow $19.99
00690384 Best of Ani DiFranco $19.95
00690322 Ani DiFranco – Little Plastic Castle $19.95
00690380 Ani DiFranco – Up Up Up Up Up Up $19.95
00690979 Best of Dinosaur Jr. $19.99
00690833 Private Investigations – Best of Dire Straits and Mark Knopfler $24.95
00695382 Very Best of Dire Straits – Sultans of Swing $22.95
00690347 The Doors – Anthology $22.95
00690348 The Doors – Essential Guitar Collection $16.95
00690915 Dragonforce – Inhuman Rampage $29.99
00690250 Best of Duane Eddy $16.95
00690533 Electric Light Orchestra Guitar Collection $19.95
00690909 Best of Tommy Emmanuel $19.95
00690555 Best of Melissa Etheridge $19.95
00690496 Best of Everclear $19.95
00690515 Extreme II – Pornograffitti $19.95
00690982 Fall Out Boy – Folie à Deux $22.99
00690810 Fall Out Boy – From Under the Cork Tree $19.95
00690897 Fall Out Boy – Infinity on High $22.95
00691009 Five Finger Death Punch $19.99
00690664 Best of Fleetwood Mac $19.95
00690870 Flyleaf $19.95
00690257 John Fogerty – Blue Moon Swamp $19.95
00690931 Foo Fighters – Echoes, Silence, Patience & Grace $19.95
00690235 Foo Fighters – The Colour and the Shape $19.95
00690808 Foo Fighters – In Your Honor $19.95
00690595 Foo Fighters – One by One $19.95
00690394 Foo Fighters – There Is Nothing Left to Lose $19.95
00690805 Best of Robben Ford $19.95
00690842 Best of Peter Frampton $19.95
00690734 Franz Ferdinand $19.95
00694920 Best of Free $19.95
00690222 G3 Live – Joe Satriani, Steve Vai, and Eric Johnson $22.95
00694807 Danny Gatton – 88 Elmira St $19.95
00690438 Genesis Guitar Anthology $19.95
00690753 Best of Godsmack $19.95
00120167 Godsmack $19.95
00690848 Godsmack – IV $19.95
00690338 Goo Goo Dolls – Dizzy Up the Girl $19.95
00690576 Goo Goo Dolls – Gutterflower $19.95
00690927 Patty Griffin – Children Running Through $19.95
00690591 Patty Griffin – Guitar Collection $19.95
00690978 Guns N' Roses – Chinese Democracy $24.99
00691027 Buddy Guy Anthology $24.99
00694854 Buddy Guy – Damn Right, I've Got the Blues $19.95
00690697 Best of Jim Hall $19.95
00690840 Ben Harper – Both Sides of the Gun $19.95
00690987 Ben Harper and Relentless7 – White Lies for Dark Times $22.99
00694798 George Harrison Anthology $19.95
00690778 Hawk Nelson – Letters to the President $19.95
00690841 Scott Henderson – Blues Guitar Collection $19.95
00692930 Jimi Hendrix – Are You Experienced? $24.95
00692931 Jimi Hendrix – Axis: Bold As Love $22.95
00690304 Jimi Hendrix – Band of Gypsys $24.99
00690321 Jimi Hendrix – BBC Sessions $22.95
00690608 Jimi Hendrix – Blue Wild Angel $24.95
00694944 Jimi Hendrix – Blues $24.95
00692932 Jimi Hendrix – Electric Ladyland $24.95
00690602 Jimi Hendrix – Smash Hits $24.99
00691033 Jimi Hendrix – Valleys of Neptune $22.99
00690017 Jimi Hendrix – Woodstock $24.95
00690843 H.I.M. – Dark Light $19.95
00690869 Hinder – Extreme Behavior $19.95
00660029 Buddy Holly $19.95
00690793 John Lee Hooker Anthology $24.99
00660169 John Lee Hooker – A Blues Legend $19.95
00694905 Howlin' Wolf $19.95
00690692 Very Best of Billy Idol $19.95
00690688 Incubus – A Crow Left of the Murder $19.95
00690544 Incubus – Morningview $19.95
00690136 Indigo Girls – 1200 Curfews $22.95
00690790 Iron Maiden Anthology $24.99
00690887 Iron Maiden – A Matter of Life and Death $24.95
00690730 Alan Jackson – Guitar Collection $19.95
00694938 Elmore James – Master Electric Slide Guitar $19.95
00690652 Best of Jane's Addiction $19.95
00690721 Jet – Get Born $19.95
00690684 Jethro Tull – Aqualung $19.95
00690693 Jethro Tull Guitar Anthology $19.95
00690647 Best of Jewel $19.95
00690898 John 5 – The Devil Knows My Name $22.95
00690959 John 5 – Requiem $22.95
00690814 John 5 – Songs for Sanity $19.95
00690751 John 5 – Vertigo $19.95
00694912 Eric Johnson – Ah Via Musicom $19.95

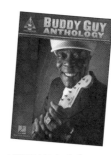

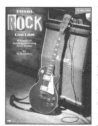